Ars Poetica and Other Poems

Ars
Poetica

and Other Poems

Stanley J. White

Beyond the Third Dimension Press

Dedicated to my daughter, Heather
and
in Memory of my wife, Ann

ISBN 978-0-9689463-2-9

www.stanjwhite.com

Contents

Acknowledgements

This book would never have been published but for the encouragement and hands-on assistance of my dear friend Bernadette Rule. I must mention two other dear friends: Becky Alexander and Katherine Gordon, with whom I have circulated my poetry for many years. I am very grateful for their encouragement. Many thanks to the members of the Arlington Seven for their valuable critiques. Thanks also go to my son-in-law, Frank, without whose IT expertise, I could never have compiled these files, and special thanks to Greg Smith of blindpigpress.

Previously published books by the author: *Four Solitudes, About Time*

Chapbooks: *Itinerant, Poems One, Annum, Anomalies of Violence, Oddities*

The following books and chapbooks were written in collaborations with various other poets: *Quaere, Portals, Telling Lies, Double Take, Seven by Seven, A Week of Thoughts, Banshee Songs*

Thanks also to the following: *The Cambridge Writers Collective, The Brantford Writers Circle, Tower Poetry, The Hamilton Poetry Centre, Byline Magazine, Serengeti Press, Craigleigh Press, Seraphim Editions.*

Foreword

This book is a collection of poems selected from 40 years of writing. The science of poetry is to translate the intangible thinking of the right brain into a familiar left brain world of matter. No attempt has been made to order the poems, either alphabetically or chronologically or by themes, in the hope that each poem will come as a surprise and maintain interest.

There are a number of poems on the subject of language throughout the book. To understand some of them, it may be necessary to have an awareness of the thought behind them. The author is passionately interested in how the presence of language influences the process of thought. Did, for instance, early societies before language, see their world as one? Does the existence of over a million words, a million labels, in our contemporary world, tend to make us think fractionally?

These poems are the tangibles of philosophies that have entered my mind over the past 92 years, and the many issues that all lives have to deal with. They are namely...an autobiography of thought.

DUET

Mostly, I live
in the world of my body.
It goes where it will,
does what it wants.

In a closer world,
unending, my mind thinks
'that's what it does'
wanders amongst stars
delights in mystery
ponders the whimsy of love.

But sometimes
it looks on, tries to make sense
of other bodies, nudges mine
one way or another, despite
impotence where comfort and
pleasure are concerned.

Nightly, sleep
takes us both away,
my body,
to nothingness
my mind,
to yet another world.

Ars Poetica

I write of stars
and of the infinity behind mirrors
and of the inconsequence of trifles

I write in the sound of the sea in shells
and of the crescendo of silence
in the light of an eye in the deep of sleep

I write between a memory and forget
in the fading half-light at the end of days

and upon the eve of every eve
I write in the epilogues of myths
of where the seaward runes once told
of when a never is born and a forever ends

I write of where an echo fades
and in the touch of a lover's hand
and of where a rainbow strays

I write in the idiom of day, daydreams
and in the sounds of tip toes in the night
and wake to a choristry of birds singing

I write in the loneliness of distant mountains
and in the thirsts of desert sands
crave the tranquility of still waters

I write in the confusion of happening
that the startled pheasant takes into the air

I write of a shoe that has never stepped
and of the hem of the emperor's clothes
and the weight of a sadness and a regret

I write in the feeling of falling fast
and in the sea-saw of the tides

I write in the crevices of dawns
and in the drone of the mumble bees
and of where a fall of wood smoke goes

I write in the synonym of time
and of the night side of the moon
and in the breath of fairy kneeling flowers
I write of stars

A Collaboration of Atoms

I am descended from infinities of universes
through the heavens that we call our own
as galaxies expanding birth a dying star
and its accoutrement a failing earth to
this dark mad and lonely city street
of yellowed dim-lit windows and
it rains in this slum alley where
I sleep alone unfriended wet
and cold and yet soon
destined to become
far less as all
needs must
I shall be
Dust

.

Early Signs of
a Very Young Poet

Moms and Dads he thought the letters,
drawn in his mother's careful hand
chalk-white on black,
the lower case, their children.

Soon, he was dotting iii's with stars,
crossing ttt's with trails of comets,
booting bouncing balls of O's
in long sighs over bars of H's.

Queries filled his mind with qqq's,
xxx'es, with mystery and censure,
and the intimate of mmm's
                    quiet moments.

He marveled
how the bbb's and ccc's and ddd's
brought swoops of sound up short
with putterings, how adding aaa's
or eee's could make sounds last,
how adding sss'es made sounds last
    forever.

Until his head was filled
with the resonance of signs,
and naps in afternoons
were sleeped in zzz's
sounding all the vowels together
in choirs of baritone bees.

Yellow Bird

It struck the windshield,
fluttered, then was gone.
I watched it dwindle
in the rearview glass
to fall a yellow asterisk
upon the road.
Had it been a sparrow
I doubt it would rate
a passing thought;
I don't know why
for both are birds,
but it was yellow
and I grieved its loss.
Perhaps it had been born
a little slower
than befits a bird
or had a more important
matter on its mind
for it was spring.
It struck the windshield
fluttered, then was gone
and I grieved its loss
   for it was yellow.

The First Poet

He felt it most deeply in the early morning
when the sun flowed softly into the mist
like a drop of water from the red-clay pool
splashed into the chalk pit, and when the tree tops
followed the sun into the whiteness of the sky.
Sometimes he felt the sun was in his head.
Sometimes, when he lay in the cave before sleep,
he thought the stars were behind his eyes.
Once, he had been caught by it
when staring into the embers of the fire
and it had taken him so far from the river,
from the cave, and so far from all that was familiar,
that he forgot his chore.
So he was given after to salting the meat,
stacking the kindling,
for he was no longer trusted with the fire
and as he worked the lowly tasks
he tried to keep the sun,
the moon, and the stars out of his head.
Until one morning gathering late berries
he rested near the still pool.
There in the pool was the sun.
The sun was in the sky and in the pool
and now the sun was in his head;
as he looked closer he saw his head was in the pool too.
It was like the patterns in the cave
but it was not the sun pictures he was seeking,

it was the music of the forest
and from his reflection he formed his mouth
to the shape of the sun and by changing its shape
he found he could mimic
the lull of the wind in the tall trees,
the screech of the night bird, the tap, tap, of rain drops,
the roar of the great river
and even the quiet of almost silence.
Taking these sounds, he placed each next to another
Until the lines lay one above the other
like two sticks in the sand.
Patiently, he made the sounds of each stick
over and over to himself until they were safely
where he kept the morning sun, where he kept the moon,
where he had kept the stars behind his eyes,
kept them safely where he visited in the embers of the fire.

Lie and Listen

The open window's nightly dawn
stirs in the weekday work-a-day breaking
under the weather, seamless, dun, sunless,
the westerly cool wind's belly rumbles
a shimmy-sharp drumming of rooftop rain
and the rained trees shiver.
Cardinals fleet their morning whim
in trifling washerwoman speak;
wet pavements spin the sweep of sounds
that rush and frush the tire-tread way
to the din of the semi's foot-floored roar
con moto falsetto the coupe, ute, sedan,
a descant ascending re-me-fa-sol-la,
and underfoot quaint, the quick and the click
dreamt in the tempt of a woman in heels.
So in the chirming, the coil, and the rouse
the calliope's note of the day streams out
to the absolute fringe of the earshot world
and the rein and the rain and the reign,
of silence.

Under a Summer's Sky

They found their Eden
between the hedgerow
and the field of golden wheat
safe from all but flying eyes.
He dressed her, as Eve.
She dressed him, as Adam.
That was all from Eden
except for the apple
which was a cherry.
She gave him, all of her
that was not of man,
and in return,
he gave her, all of him
that was not of woman.
It was dusk before they left,
leaving only their nakedness,
 and the cherry.

Spring Cleaning the Old Manse

Memories are common as cobwebs
and in the corners of the entrance hall
we find residues of well-wishes
left perhaps by guests before leaving.
In the dining room,
festooned about a chandelier,
is a gallimaufry of hopes and longings
which we bag and put out to waste.
The scullery is cheery enough
but for one regret, so large
as to take two of us to carry it out.
And in an upstairs bedroom
Esther finds the remnants
of a child's cry which she could not
bring herself to throw out
but later treasured in a sandalwood box.
A carpet in the drawing room
is stained and ruined by dried sorrows
where we sweep promises, expectations,
and disappointments into neat piles.
Jeremy re-appears staggering
under the weight of a peal
of dark brown laughter
which he had found in the attic.

And in the summerhouse after,
Jennifer discovers a trove of love
and several bushels of kisses
which she trowels into the flower beds.
Excellent for roses, she says.

The Locksmith's Tale

From Minterne Magna I was come
on my way to Godmanstone.
By Kettle Bridge I stopped
and sought the manor
that I might some menial task perform
in recompense for victuals
and in due turn was asked
what manner was my trade.
I was employed I say
of master Heppelthwaite of Berwick
by business of grapple, clinch
sneck, lock and any fastenings.
Odd mindly as my telling told
gave of more than passing interest
and much whispering of maid
such that I was taken thus anon
to My Lady's private chamber
where she stood but in her
wanton curve cotehardie top
and bottomed only in that
which I was taxed with un-affixing
and so I took my mastery
to such a simple lock
as to guard such exquisite of value
for though I could have let it in a trice
so in dawdled time I must admit
to tempt of trifled un-necessity

for there was much pleasantry
in my thoroughness
till listening as is my wont
its tumblers tripped;
My Lady's loosed impediment
fell impotently at her feet.
Give him ale, give him bread,
a capon, a baron of beef,
a leg of lamb, My Lady joyed
and I was taken to the kitchens
and duly feted with sufficient
for my journey and then back

and so I left not accustomed
to so happenstance of afternoons;
I thought an end to such diversion
and put a brace of miles behind me
till under an old moon
hence-ward, I heard a hurry of horses,
two, and a livery man
who bade me mount and follow
forth headlong to the manor's pother
and hustle without ceremony again
directly to My Lady's chamber.
Oh what a different countenance
she now bestowed worsen for her wine
and from her shamble, license
my late talent had afforded her.
I gave attention to the dire necessity.

Her maids with frantic bustle did re-bot
and deftly with my pick relocked its lock
and so My Lady's treasure was
once more ensconced and she endowed
with virtues of the saint and nun.
Then without concupiscence I left
taking to the woods and fields
far of the bridle path His Lordship passed
in coterie of knights on his return.
I hurried, put my distances to night
for I lacked certainty in those
who might, in pique, betray My Lady's trust
for I was much in fear His Lordship
might seek reward of me for services.

An Art Collector

It began as a hobby
but as time went on
it became an addiction.
My wife complained
she didn't know
where we might store them all.

It was windows, you see.
Every time I would see a window
with a wonderful view
I would purchase it.
I now have several hundred.
Those I particularly like,
I have had framed.

One of a starry night
we hang on the bedroom wall.
So often have I been dependant
on the sailor's star.
Its nearness is so very comforting.
A night sky with a full moon
I keep covered since my wife
finds the light keeps her awake.

I have several windows
with wonderful views of mountains
and the lure of green wilderness
stretching to horizons.
They are pleasant keepsakes
of great loveliness, though
we must remember never to go there
for it will inevitably break the spell.

Foolishly, I bought a window
of a New York City street
not realizing that the noise
would drive us up the wall.
Finally I had to store it in the shed
at the bottom of the garden
but then the neighbours complained,
so I buried it deep in a flowerbed.
In rush-hours it can still be heard faintly
if you put your ear to the ground.

Seascapes or large areas of water
can be a problem due to the humidity
and the danger of a tsunami.
We had a problem with one that surprised us
with an unexpectedly high tide.
Also, I avoid snow scenes. Heating bills
can become increasingly expensive.

My favourite is a view of a small,
angelic looking boy playing happily
with pebbles on the banks of a lazy river.
The man said it was the Christ Child.
I've no reason to disbelieve him
for the window came
from a hovel in Guatemala.

Thought of Art of Thought

Yesterday I saw your thoughts again
set down in oil on canvas
each trimmed with a tinge of rainbows.
One left your brush in umber
to form the stature of a tree.
Another in careful consideration
laid itself down in the sunlight
of an amethyst stream
touched imperiously with wine.
Yet another, an after-thought perhaps,
edged the meandering path
with a daydream of chartreuse.
I see the doubt of procrastination
and the eventual touch
of depression in your shadows—
a Payne's grey and your sky so desolate,
reminiscent of sad memories I suspect.
And is the lone bird...a lost lover?
Yet in the twirl
of your joyful thoughts of grasses
I sense your muses dancing.

Strange how similar your thoughts,
to those of friends' who think in words,
                    who think in music!

Salmagundi

Out of the labyrinth of time
from nothingness I come and go
as all and everything:
Lucretius, the little match girl,
seven seraphim on a conch shell,
Leonidas of Sparta,
the young woman on Sandymount Strand;
all of everything I am, I was, I will be
      and there is more:
for I am a fragment of the Taj,
prayer in the temple of Artemis,
spindrift from the Mull of Kintyre,
a dot over an "i" in Wind in the Willows.
I am scent of chervil, taste of angelica
and wherefore the art of Romeo and Juliet.
I am the paintings in the mind of Raphael,
a smudge of Tyne coal on an urchin's cheek,
the light from every candle
and a black heart well worn on a sleeve
for I am ever the all of everything
      even the dust of stars

Heart

The ball stopped inches from my hand.
Was I throwing or catching?

Vacuum stilled the wind
pencilling birds in flight.
Seas stalled in their breakers.
Iron stopped rusting,
and pause caught
planets and stars standing.

There was no fanfare,
everything quietly stopped,

like the ball inches from my hand.
Was I throwing or catching?

A Taste of Summer

I remember that long summer of doves
out of a gymslip lisle blue stockings
home weatherless for the holidays
to a sky filled also blue with nothingness
and a sun august heaving in a ripple heat

so when he came seemingly from never
on the way to somewhere, so he said,
we walked that day and talked
along the sands over the sea-sound surf
of what might be talked about
up to Oxford next year Balliol he said, and you?
perhaps, I said, the year after—
talked of where and when, and so he stayed

and on this other day we touched, just lips,
my first and lovely and forever after
and so he stayed and later on we walked
in amongst the soft warm round of dunes
touching and feeling the fine sand
running through the fingers of salt grasses,
my first and ever after memory

and/or of the likely that he would not leave,
for the pearl of bliss lay scheming in the quick of us,
we walked and talked along the Folly Clough
the seed-shaped river steeped between high bluffs
where over the gabble of the water falling
we romped the shingled shore in halfling joy
witting soft beneath the rise of statue rock
about sweet everythings touching and touching
more until we more than touched
where the river's eddies ran through pothole-deeps
to the sanctuary of the sea

and for that far somewhere once he came
he left and the dovey'd summer rained
and in a puzzle of tears the blue skies fell
leaving my first and ever everything
                              to memory after

Windfalls

I cherish skies, the creativity of clouds,
prize the wilderness its emptiness
and bow to noons and afternoons. I
court the night and muse the mysteries
of its moons, praising the slight of
amber on fall leaves and all that glows,
in awe of hanging icicles from eaves, to
the emerging corn in rows that conjure
fields' burnt umber's turn to ochre
until the summer yields to winter's
broker and its diamond snows
delighting in a world of silent quiet
that sets a snowfield's tranquil glaze
antipodal of a summer's riot as is
September's evening breeze. I treasure
dawns, the twittering of birds lauding the
remnants of the night and in the silence
left by words, murmured in a candle's light,
I crave the ever-coming of the days
tomorrow's unexpected rain's surprise
and all the weather's ways that bring
the winter's spring again, the fall's return,
and summers, some as if they were forever
as if the Earth were turning just for me,
as though it shall be over...never.

Martini Song

Is this all there is?
or so the song is sung
by those who have not
rested in the shade of angels,
who stumble through a whisky world
taking the long way round a short stay.

What manner of masturbation is this?
Put these words straight
so they read, in Korean if you must,
like instructions for a garden shed
or Do-It-Yourself bookshelves
but make them sound—
I-s t-h-i-s a-l-l t-h-e-r-e i-s?

Let the world speak for itself
sunsets are the sun's soliloquies,
neap tides the urge of a love's seduction.
And that quiet always of an uneventful day,
a woman's love.

Life does not speak in undertones
        of cloistered nuns,
in whispers of a trauma spoken of in shame.

Leave your heart out
on a wet slab in the hot sun;
cry for the wonder of another's day.

Damn your philosophies—
their imaginings.
It is the feel of things,
the seconds, the minutes bringing
on the monsoon of a Time's surprise

hot chocolate in a blue December,
blush of a spring morning
shadow-pink upon a whitening wall;
love in the shade of an August noon,
returns from long journeys to familiar beds,

fresh surprises ever new unfolding
in the feel of things
that beat and beat
upon the tin, tin, tin, tin,
tin roof of the soul—
That's all there is!

Take a Field for Instance...

left as a parcel of memory
touch of your fingers
on a leaf of dock
smell of mown-hay
hayseed taste of its stems
the sound of water
moving anywhere
a hush of breath
as the wind tousles,
and how the sun pictures it
on a summer's day
But there's more
that defies description
It's why you want to go back
take your girl
if only you knew where

On Opening an Encyclopedia

She would have passed unnoticed in any crowd
not even the merest hint her left breast,
like an atlas globe, pictured the world
as it was in the sixteenth century, her other,
the craters on the moon, I recognized Vendelinus.
On her back, draped as though from her shoulder
the complete text of the Rosetta Stone
followed by a Hebrew prayer
and on her belly, fully illustrated, a page
from the *Book of Kells* and several cave paintings.
Elsewhere a plethora of names: Pythia, Hadwijch
Baba Vanga, Abe Ro Seimei, Therese of Lisieux
and a quotation from Nostradamus.
In the middle of her back, an equation
appeared to solve a riddle of the quantum...
a foreign tongue told the fate
of the crew of the *Mary Deare*
and an account of the history of the *Amistad* natives.
In a place somewhat hidden from view
some tiny modest diagrams from the *Kama Sutra*
and a portrait of Grigori Rasputin
all in the midst of mysterious clefs of an unknown symphony.
Such was the magnanimity of the outpouring of knowing
that it overflowed onto her upper arms and down her thighs.
Only one small panel of ivory flesh remained untouched
an inch or two above her navel.
She was keeping it, she said, for the epitaph of a lost lover.

After an Early Photograph
of Brighton Pier

In the breath between words
the trip between steps
the skip between heartbeats,
out of all eternity, one moment split,
preserves beyond their time
their shapes and shadows, their affairs
and even hats and parasols
(we will not argue about souls).

A dot amidst dots out of stars;
what chance coincidence
drew them to the sea's calling
on this day commonplace,
early afternoon, a sun's warming
called them from the city;
what miracle of whereabouts and when
in Time's hiatus touched their immortality?

Under the anaesthesia of the afternoon
unknowing of lost likenesses now stored
as preserved appendices in formaldehyde,
oblivious, they go about aboutnesses
remote in orderly reserve
polite, detached, needing to conform;
deliberate, each step a careful step
unhurried, even children.

Not unlike a dream, the scene's
beyond unerring recollection,
vague reminiscences of spectres seen
who frequent seaweed-salty smells,
the seagull sounds, the siffle of the surf,
and heedless, in continuums of happening,
people who might be us,
might be me, might be you.

Tonight in boarding houses,
promenade hotels, devious couples pose
as seemly Mr. and Mrs. Smith.
Under Victorian skirts the weekend
London lovers come, for this is Brighton.
The old too, husbands and wives who have
summered here for fifty years, and those
who come just once from nowhere and alone.
Strangely their joys and sorrows show:
children hand in hand and dressed in white,
a child that smallpox or consumption takes,
young man's proposal to young woman's joy,
old man's journey to the sea for one last time.

Is there a child, as yet unborn though
recently conceived, shall live a hundred years
and run the gauntlet of your stars?

Of a Heavy Thought

I am afraid of a world
she will no longer be
a world that cannot
accommodate her
(or accommodate me)
afraid that the mornings
shall never reach noon
that each day fail the sun
each night fail the moon
and that all of the seasons
shall roll into one
and every day wither
once she has gone.

Li Po 2014 A.D.

Do I need to listen
to whoever they are
whatever they say
deliberating on the state
of their latest war
talking of what gold
has gone into which pocket
obsessing over
the dreams of idols
telling of cloud for tomorrows
and the perpetual stupidities
for the days and for the hours
of peopled events?

Do they want from me sadness
or that I should set down my word?
      —what is this to me
who sits beside a wood
in the company of a rosy wine,
the moon, and fireflies

A Time

The old, old, man
drinks enough wine
to leave his body behind
only ever useful
to a woman
and now she's gone

but his mind is left
in the threat
of imminent thunder,
with an image where
marked in the middle
of a field, he holds
his metal walking cane
high above his head.

There is a time
when a man
must have faith in God.

Rosetta Stone

See, I put my long-gone
sounds to lexicon
not the faintest echo now
page-silent ever
in a longtime space
this bottled genie
waiting for the rub of read
Then for an instant back
to fleeting sound again
you sing my song

Equality of Night

In this drunken juggling of spheres
time in no time the sidereal of days,
this gyre of gipsy tipsy worlds
that salt the seasons in a clock-long now
—this equilux of equinox and sister solstice
a peal of bells that chime the turning time
and start or separate the hand-fast seasons
yet promulgate the pagan festivals.
Their heirs shall grace the Christian flam.

The Celts, the Druids knew the jugglery
of drawing down the sun (the moon),
short on long shadows and shadowless
in circle flare of megalithic cairn and henge:
these were the eves and days of pagan lore,
sun sports of civil twilights, civil dawns
in which Pleiades and the planets star
the brinks of All Souls, Hallow and Lammas
and all cross quarter days of Candlemas.

These lives held of beliefs in slivers of the sun:
Three Souls, Black Heart of Innocence,
and the Pentacles of Iron and Pearl.
Will those who glory in their Celt descent,
remember singing, dancing, in this wind
that blows about the faeryland of feri-wicca fey
that came with all the niceties of vice and sacrifice
down failing years in bard and mantic privilege?
Behold this veil of words, in wonder of this world!

A Presence of Mind

Much as I love my Canada,
I spend my fading days vicariously
among the fields of an English countryside.
From the window of the cottage
I delight in the many songs of a trout stream
and the presence, in walking distance, of
a rise, once a hill-fort and the century's signs
of a later ruin thought to be Norman.
A wood with two owls borders the hills
where, close by, are badgers
and, in the oxbow pool, a water rat.
I have made friends with a hedgehog;
in the evenings I leave milk out for him.
No dwellings for miles ensure the solitude,
though in my dreams I converse with shepherds
from whom I learned the Saxon word
                              for longing.

Valentine

I did come back, you know,
alone, one February night
in the choke of winter,
the street, rain-black, slick
as oilcloth. Street lights danced.

Across the narrow darkness
a gauntlet of row-houses
bowed to each in deference
and blocks away the streetcars
snarled another world.

And off the sidewalk
brownstone steps,
the cast iron railing
I remembered as a boy,
I looked up
at your lighted window
                              and the door
            I dared not open.

Tundra Green

Sun had breakfast elsewhere
on this Thursday
out of a blue wind tinged
with Wednesday's wood smoke
                    drawn
on an ice-wine cool
and arctic menthol
seasoned with disco leaves
in a blender's helix
                    under
the belly'd clouds
the grey on greyness
the snow-feel sky blown day
the colour of warfare
                    she
stumbles the frozen furrows
to Hudson's inlet
for flour granola pasta
and a pink bow
                    knows
what he had said
in a fit of drinking
soon it would be
too hazardous to leave him

The Tower of Padrat

Its door shall be found only by she
who gravid lost too early child to night
and talks of wild roses now and shadow
Soon ghillie shoes shall decorate her feet
and sundial shells adorn her hair
Dress her in woven petals of nightshade
leaving one breast free for the cephalenes
Let her carry the clavis hidden at her thighs
Follow a full moon at a neap tide ebb
and lest she loses sightings in her quest
sprinkle sequins in her wake like stars

Enlightenment

When I was out time-travelling one day
I set down in a prehistoric bay
to strike a conversation with a man
as those who speak Neanderthal can

I said I hope you do not think me rude
but may I help you with the crude ideas
you have about your world
(before the banner of the sciences is unfurled)?

I told him there is not much remarkable about the sun
that even copulation is not simple fun
and all about the birds and bees
how similar principles apply to trees

that lakes and rivers are nothing but H^2O
and why his breath facilitates combustion when he'll blow
that volcanoes have little to do with deities
even showed by the moon and stars what day it is

and using pi unravelled all the mysteries of the wheel
explained to him when he's depressed just how he'll feel
but I left with a most distinct impression
that he did not appreciate the lesson

Ten Green Bottles

One was found on Calvary half-filled
      with vinegar
Another came from Socrates
                —the dregs of hemlock

A third with love-note, ship, and genie
      owned by Sinbad

The fourth, a small vial "Drink Me" left by Alice

A fifth keeps remnants of a Life's Elixir

And a sixth the wine from
      Days of Wine and Roses

Seven a Brangaene potion
love-charmed Tristan und Isoldte mad

An eighth found hidden neath a tapestry within
      Lucretia's house

The ninth holds Hyde and Jekyll's formula

And the tenth and last was used
      to fill the Holy Grail

                —all left hanging on the wall

Brume at Vespers

Before the interim of night
on the heels of a day of rain
that cools the earth in aftermath
the breath of condensate
has leveled hollows
the sky has fallen
lies forlorn mute windless
hedge-height across the fields
close touchless silent
in a gloom of grey
a white vignette all silhouette
gossamer-veiled diaphanous
this vista drawn of tiers
in dusks of zebra'd hue
a sigh of light in all its subtlety
until so exquisitely touched
by the brush of darkness

When musing on a consideration of Proust's: *In Search of Lost Time* or *Remembrance of Things Past*

There it was—heavy stuff,
so the thought never carried
past a half a dozen feet
before falling to the ground
where I was careful not to step on it.

Yet your average thought
will carry easily across a room
where most strike the wall
and fall to the baseboard.
Thousands are vacuumed up every day.

Outdoors, they are more fun to watch:
like pages of newspaper
caught in local eddies of rising air;
up and up they go, like my thought
of Peter Rabbit
          treasured from childhood;
light as gossamer...it went on rising,
until out of curiosity, a bird circled it
and it disappeared forever into a cloud.

Sense Less

I was told by one shadow
that my house had a pointed roof
and later, by another, that it did not
Both were messengers of the sun
who were like blind men
trying to describe an elephant

At Ninety-One

This sadness,
of blood, flesh, and bone
ravaged by years
can still feel the wind
taste the wine
feel the warmth of the sun
as though it were the touch
of a woman, even savour the
feel of how moonlight
charms the darkness;
it still marvels at how
Mozart tailored noise to
make sound an ecstasy
and how the vision of
a cloud might touch
a moment in its
possessions of the past
where it once knew love

for most of its today is yesterday
and all of its tomorrow is today

Driving North on a Winter's Evening

The night lowers its grey veil
over the sky giving preference
to the fields, their patchwork
of dying snow sullied now
with a late mist of rain that
in the hue of blue-black grape
softens the trees to idle smoke.
The road, now an arrowhead,
points the distance darkening,
as bright burning lights from
peopled rooms in random farms
dot about the wilderness of hills
reminding of day and of work,
and all that of night is oblivious.
Yet the dark, the hour, persist
demanding a space, a time—
the importance of a remembrance.

Used Parts

In my little finger is an atom
I'm not sure which
that once was part of Genghis Khan
and another in my earlobe
is from Marie Antoinette
from when she scratched an itch
   In my elbow are iota
   that once had been a part
   of the Mona Lisa's smile
and in my toe (the one with arthritis)
an unmentionable fragment
   of a noted Soho tart
Every time I take a breath
I wonder who has breathed it first
a warthog in Abyssinia
a consumptive dung beetle in Virginia
   it bothers me that my other bits
at least once have all been used before
and most considerably more
Should I eat this celery that might
contain a pinch of ling?
 In this potato chip
   is there a mite of pterodactyl wing?

It's a miracle that I work so well
made up of so many antiquated pieces
which I don't even own—
          all of them on leases
My mother who was particularly clean
would have said oh don't pick him up
you never know where he might have been

A Windfall Fall

Out of the blind of his mother's womb, into the revel of breath
he falls through the one long day.
                   The ever-rending night
                         reminds of fetal dark—
                              its shadow always at his shoulder.

The opiate of youth his burden,
in free fall seasons through a gravity of days to years' ellipsis.
Anguish he carries where idyll slipped away
under the spinning hay-make sun that weaves his shroud

until his velvet touch turns to the game of heads;
mace in the marrow, aspic in the vein,
patina on the antique nerve
       carries the stars away,
       quiets birdsong,
       tames wild strawberries.

Under his rouge of words, his go—
                         a weather wavering.

Who Loves a Rainy Night?

You need a city for a rainy night;
it is nothing without street lamps,
reflections in wet pavement.
You need sound too—
traffic in the distance, streetcars
and a rain not too wet
but with puddles well established,
you will walk hurriedly
raindrops tapping out a rhythm
to your footsteps, returning late
on an arm, snuggled into a shoulder
coming back from somewhere
you had looked forward to
       and will now remember.

You, the Owl, and the Moon

The moon followed you home last night
—you with the head full of stars
and the bottle of Opney's—
followed you out of the breath of sky
from the far side of the trees
keeping her distance
saw you turn at Galagher's farm
all of a sudden spinning on your heel
at the owl's hooting

    ...this was the world:
        you, the owl, and the moon...

but she was too swift for you,
and stopped and looked away
as though you were of no interest,
not until you turned again, she turned,
watched you wrestle with thickets
leaf your way through the Weald Wood;
the yard gate took you two falls out of three

All night she watched you secondhand
through your window,
drifting, mellow, behind your eye,
followed the hour-hand down the wall
till the Earth turned on the both of you
and the agony of the sun itself
filled your head

Dear Editor

I am sending you an early poem
which I am sorry to say
has suffered badly
from the passage of years.
You will note all the verbs
in the present tense of the original
are now in the past:
is'es are now was'es
are's are now were's
and in the first stanza
the words 'polished table'
are barely readable
under a thick layer of dust.
In the second,
the energetic lady hiker,
who had no difficulty
in bounding up and down hills
and vaulting streams
at the time the poem was written,
is now scarcely able to navigate
without the use of a walker
and help from her husband—
the gentleman in the third stanza
with the long beard and deerstalker cap.
I assure you, the mouldy
half-eaten sandwich tossed casually
into the aspidistra (verse 3, 4th line)

was not there in the original poem
and I have done my best
to clean up the crumbs.
Be assured, I have vacuumed the poem
from beginning to end.
It is, in the main, now quite sanitary
though I would advise against
opening the door of the refrigerator
you will find in the last line
of the penultimate stanza.
                    Cordially,
                        Yours, etc., etc.

Feral Child

They struck within, without warning,
sought to leave no witness, yet the child unnoticed
watcher and silent weeper in the wood,
saw in the hour, a day, a year of fear until
they left him to return to drying blood and flies,
to lie and cry, for love of kin and inconsolable
until the carrion came frightening.
Grave and grave-less he watched, wary
from the haven of the hill
for this was an un-peopled time
distanced from safe hamlets by a span of moons.

Fortune was the season of the sun
the petal-shed and berry'd season
and so he hungered on the risk of trial,
suffered the belly'd agony of error
gnawed on the bones of carrion kill
catching, on occasion, birds, a vole,
strayed carp from a shallow pool;
lived on hoppers, cress from streams,
ran a savage gauntlet raw;
frail from craze of hunger,
grief of loss and loneliness.

Fall-caught in the first and unclad cold.
Ransacked rank carcasses for fur, for warmth,
hand-raked the fall of leaves to eiderdown,
sheltered ill from the wind in stony clefts,
shivered in sleet beneath umbrella pine.
Then in deep of winter, falling in with wolves,
slept in a dark and toasty den,
supper'd on plagues of mice, ice wined.
Till winter lost its spring and spring its winter,
the stoned earth reeled toward the sun
leaving at large the star-cold watered snows.

By seasons, sun by moon, the land
would take him to her breast—
return him to the bosom of old time told
where summer taught the skills of early men
of trap and sling, cunning of beasts,
knowing each flower and herb and seed
but not by word-by provender or bane,
for in return she took his early sounds
of speak and shout and whisper,
left to him the baying of the wolf
for praying to the gods unknown to men.

The seasons made their fancies free in fall,
footloose on winter-windy crags
moving by hill-stream, forest-shore, in spring,
barefoot-easy ran their thorny summers.
Knowing the taste of roasted flesh but once
by accident of fire the forest filled his belly.
Until a year of different hunger—
age of engendered gender's need;
unknowing, craved the rush of seed
a mania that women klept
breath-less as in a cat's failed preying.

And so the intrigue of all life he lived,
short living through a sinlessness of seasons,
his tongue the feral sounds of fox-bark, bear,
boy-lover and kin of wolf.
Hinted by travellers from a glimpse imagined?
Rumoured in distant inns as if a myth or god,
un-bothered by conundrums of mankind,
no more the wherefore or the wise of man,
his life no more account than roach or brier
lived and died without the burden of identity,
fearing the scent and treachery of men.

Music

What form you have
your miscellany of patterns
fills my mind with
the gossamer of your sadness,
the ebullience of your joy.
What curiosity of sound
engenders such serendipity
...language of birds,
dances of silence?

Augustus

Forgive this slip of continents
for this is England's turn so
bear with me and flip these pages
to a childhood journal's day.
Once and only once each year we
left from Brummagem and smoke
to where the seaside waves
and meets the Aberdovey shore.
August Bank Holidays and sun
the fab of family now all gone
yet then we waded plashed
amongst the River Dovey's trout
tripped to Cader Idris,
Betws-y-coed, Borth,
and supped on flounder,
fresh from Tal-y-bont, and chips.
These were the ecstasies
I measured all my future living by.

Thoughts on the Border of Neurosis

Co-ordinates

Picture a line to represent perception
that intersects the beam of memory's projection
and at that point but in a third dimension
imagination's line of intervention
making an asterisk—a twinkling star
that marks precisely where you are.

Rorschach

Wide as all imagination
Long as the memory of the earth
Pregnant with the reveries of all creation
Ink Blot
Perish the thought I have—you are God!

Nature of Myth

When, of every other loch I know much less
How come I know so much about Loch Ness?
On account of something that might not exist
Makes me wonder just what else I've missed.

Responsibilities

I wish that god would send
some indication of where I end
for I can avoid so many sins
if I could know where I end
and the world begins

A Little Knowledge

As a child I was reconciled
to the concept of infinity.
Then I learned to count from one to ten
and never comprehended infinity again.

The Nature of Abstraction

Sometimes a wild thought comes to me
and strikes a bargain with reality
enough to set my senses reeling.
I should have left it as a feeling.

Cognitive Dissonance

There is a part of me
which needs inform
another part of me.
If it's deceived
which part am I?

Foundations

Like a cloud
the future hangs.

The present stands
on shifting sands.

Only the past
is built to last

Cart Before The Horse

How many times have you heard the line
"Oh My Lord, is that the time?"
as though experience needs revision
to keep in step with a clock's precision

Worry Wort (A. cynanchicha)

Primrose, wisley pink, clematis
comfrey, honeysuckle, phlox
purslane, catchfly, purple loosestrife
larkspur, tansy, hollyhocks

When a summer turns to autumn
every flower needs to know
was it blooming as an annual,
prays to God it can't be so

Need for Charms

touch the age now living
on the edge of breath
that follows the faith
of nature's easy curve
as casual as sofa sex
but yet I add
for certainty in part
a grain of sand
from the vein
of an offal heart

trust a dove-day's promise
in a month of wolves
that ushers in black widow time
yet has no truck with mimsy talk
too soon the garlic Sundays leave
with lilty girls and alban wine
but in case
my reasoning should fail
I add *thieves' vinegar*
and *head of a coffin nail*

live the fable of the cave
in the idle quiet of dark
feast on all that tastes of salt
and from the sea
drink of moon milk xanthic
and in a lifetime's tidy wake
the valkyries should smile on me
but lest you deem this witless
I add a night of *angel's dark*
and *Madame Geneva's witness*

who cannot spare an instant of
the present for the past
lays the hourglass on its side
that cannot hold off sleep
much less than death
don't tempt me with a half-moon tide
or I shall challenge fate
give it more than it can handle
cinquefoil, black salt
four quarter candle

The Trapper's Wife

I watched you from the window of my heart
leaving before the winter occupied the town
Across Medaska field I watched, beyond the tower,
beyond the sawmill's termite-sawdust mound.
Infantry man with pack on pack, you walked
leaning into the weight of middle distance,
your standard, the antenna of your rifle.
North you footed past the cottage playground
past lakes accessible in reach of city trifles
to where, way-out in spring we'd watched
from Coney mountain
across a baize of pine and spruce—
a green broom sweep to cliffs a weekend walk away
that river'd on eleven days to Black Bear Falls
and Ryderman's ramshackle cabin where
they found all three that twenty's spring
stiff for want of winter game, and still as oxbow.

When April thaws do not forget
to burn wet cedar on your fire
    and I shall join you.

When I Leave

I shall think that time is leaving
that I shall freeze
in the middle of writing an "I"
that in the need of happen
there will be no falling stars.
The moon will summon a tide
to her apron string;
nowhere will there be a sunrise.

Where there is light
a woman will pause
before planting a rose.
Where there is dark
a child will be sleeping.

Somewhere, I shall be,
                    unknowing.

Prestidigitation

How we yearn
for cause without effect,
effect without cause—
clouds without rain,
to walk on water,
inexplicable reversal
of the inevitable.

Likes of Houdini fudged it,
and the bare soles
that walk across hot coals
not to mention prayer
not to mention hope.
Yet the best god will do
is to offer us luck.

The Sandman Falls
for Amelia

He takes a bagged supper and flask of tea,
waits for her rapid eye movements
now sits in the rattan chair
she has thoughtfully left
at the entrance to her occipital lobe
the most pleasant of atria,
softly lighted, had her eyes been open.
He is used to feeling an intruder—
for nobody invites the dreamer.

Avoiding her fears—
the stuff of nightmares,
he goes directly to her hopes,
the usual: detached, three-bedroom,
two-car, garage, two and a half children.
Modest, but for the prospect of diva
where a brief examination of her
medial prefrontal cortex
suggests far from perfect pitch.

He does not pry into her past—
too many unpleasant surprises.
Eating his sandwich, careful of crumbs,
exits her memory except to lay
three gentle nudges side by side:
an idea for a poem on doting children,
and two cheeky thoughts she would not
thank him for sharing with you.
On the rattan chair, before she wakes,
he leaves a dozen long stemmed roses.

Research & Development

Think of it as a huge room filled with drafting tables
pencil sharpeners, a time-clock, book-in, book-out,
   take a sick day!
And a thousand, thousand, thousand blueprints.
One, a late improvement of a squirrel modified
   to find its nuts,
another to correct a fatal flaw in lemmings, and
the redesign of several moths for less attraction
   to a candle flame.
Tucked in a corner, seldom mentioned,
a cabinet of shallow drawers contains the drafts of dinosaurs.
And treated with great honour and respect, a single blueprint
framed and hanging on the wall—the cockroach.

Today, they're working on a rush job to effect
some changes to a curious genus that surprised them all
by walking on two legs and laughing.
No upgrades for a century or two the records show,
since some apprentice draftsman, for a lark,
had tinkered with a gene in missionaries
that turned the species' love life upside down.

How to keep them ticking in their overcrowded world—
a pinch less of omnipotence, an extra humble-gene?
A tablespoon of estrogen, a little less progesterone?
Perhaps a modicum of innocence from a sleeping child?
Some magical elixir that makes them think One God—
    but which?
With an enormous sigh the architect
inscribed a line through umpteen crosses and a naught
    then ran his fingers through his hair, and wept.

A Ninety-First Autumn

In the dreamery of hills
the autumn best returns
from summers' greens
the readied maple ripe
amongst the citrus hues
soft in the morning mist
as though behind
a breath on glass
that warming sun
by afternoon transforms
as though a sunset settles
    on the woods
filling the eye with
         wonderment.

Dictionary

Tome-smug, self-satisfied,
it sits upon the table,
each-every single poem
ever written, in its pages;
its next word unforeseen
clevers a single couplet
whatever that might be—
some obscure utterance:
beath, jaggery, jalapin
moory, fenestellid, flam,
dekadarchy, bishopstool,
meeth, equæval, manticor.
It's up to the task and more
and tempts me with its
tongue-roll, lip-smack
antic belfry sounds
filling the silences with
bafflegab and serendipity.
This fancy lettered god
holds all the mysteries of life
—mind-gold for those
who make coherent order
from its incomprehensible.

Collecting Herbs on the Road to Heaven

In peasant words, I was sent by the emperor to Chang-tu.
Taking the only road by way of Szechwan,
we pass through the city of weeds
over the Chin barrier where six dragons
                         revolve around the sun.
Here to pick herbs under an evening moon
among the empty hills beneath Kao Pao.
We give the emperor new life.
There are many who are fond of the immortals.
                         The path is steep.
We leave the horses in favour of eagles.
On our return the white-headed crows cry.
At Ts'an Tsung Bridge the floods take the horses
their burdens lost, leaving us with less than stars.
We swallow our groans and turn again towards Tai Pa.
Now, we shall not return until after the festival of Wu.
    Lo Fu will be waiting for me at the fortune gate.

Reruns

Anywhere in time
a night without weather
commonplace
a lull between happenings
here perhaps
or somewhere
that might be anywhere
and someone—
you perhaps, or me
or someone, say,
across oceans
centuries ago

maybe Plato,
Mary Magdalene,
Livy or Li Po
or someone I know
or that you remember
or perhaps an
unknown peasant
at the close of a long day—

walking...
no... no ...standing,
alone... yes... alone,
yes, that's it:
someone standing alone
near still waters—

the same chill
the same dark
the same moon
the same thought

Night Drive from the Sault in Summer

Into half a world of darkness to meet the sun
                              —not need, but novelty
a drive towards a spindling star a night away
to meet the city's morning.
Leaving the trappings of the town,
drabs of outskirts, corner stores and car lot corners.
Macadam, the wheels demand,
laid upon ten-thousand years of nomad tracks.

The road is lonely.
No one travels through the night.
The day's for driving.
How quiet the Earth wheels on its bearings now
only the wind and the noise of man,
the reassuring drum of drive and tire
tacking a seam through darkness.

This sigh of sound in silence through opened windows
disturbs the quiet of those who lie awake and fret
and passes silent through a thousand dreams
   of those who sleep.

Headlights throw their fingering webs upon the
    braille of trees.
The highway glides behind the eye, beside the ear—
fleet images that brush the canvas of the eye.
Fishes and flora catch the breath of fields.
A flimsy tracing skimps complexity
cuts to the memory of the writer's word.

Beyond the turn to Chapleau, a finger's span of wilderness
where a fuel line freeze one season spelled disaster,
stop signs give the unpaved tracks regard,
nibble at the hinterland to nowhere—
bear country, coma of night in wild places;
lakes: Endikai, Webskwasheshi, Sinaminda,
under the same moon.

With these deep sighs and sough of sound they pass,
follow the road,
a kernel in the womb of light the shape of teardrops.
The dark, a withywind, the lake its shoulder.
The light's brief fingers paint the fall of waking dreams,
glimpse the failures, café closed, the boarded store
and houses derelict in fields the bush reclaimed.
Yet still the children prosper reared in downturn time
and wonder all that happens in the dark
through villages no more than a slight thickening of life—
so many worlds, so many people, even love.
Peripheral, an instant man falls from the corner of an eye
(a ghost perhaps) before the gates of night
    close silently behind.

There is a distance to this time of morning
as though the Earth withdraws.
The mind is turned toward eternity.
For the living, these are the hours of dying,
no time for levity, the gravity of life is weakening;
the windows blind, in houses sleep
where wind is thickened by the dark.
Only the signs that signify the curves
and still the yellow line divides the eye.

An elbow turn about the lake on Huron's shoulder,
the blackened greens that forest fires might leave,
burrow the night-dark, south now,
count down of backward miles till morning
birl on the planet's bearing toward the sun,
the highway running endless past the eye.
The pattern of exhaust, the huff of tires,
the dash's reassuring fingers, comfort.

Down through the brie of cottages
and phony islands of the displaced city,
the darkness ebbing, scurries westward.
The tide of light in flood flows up the eastern shore.
Road rivers flow into the delta of the morning,
into the outskirt spread of trivia,
the filigree of city sound, the hi-tech trespass, sci-fi steal—
shrapnel from the detonated city
falls in strident colours once respectable by night.

And this infinitesimal of journeys,
then, but neither *here* nor now—
this passing Eden of no significance,
out of nowhere and lost in life,
fraught as thistle seed upon the wind
written in a century's habit of trite words
in strophe, stroke and serif, space and line,
(common as runes in Cynewulf's time)
almost beguiles the fragile page.

Questions...

How can I leave music behind
How can I leave words that
kneel at the feet of stars
How can I leave dreams of love
where ecstasy's at the touch of a finger
How can I leave your canvas
of distant hills where
your sun has left its brush of autumns
How can I leave the warmth I feel
in the presence of friends
...the memories of when my life
was graced with spring flowers

Take of me what you will
but leave at least my reminiscence

Poem of a Rainy Day

For the past week
I have been trying to figure
how to put down
a wet morning, on paper—
how to capture that
translucent shoe box
experience of the drab,
the uncomfortable,
how to bring the clouds
low enough for that feeling
of falling yet not so low
as to interfere with the eraser
on the end of my pencil.
I have had the adjectives
and nouns ready
for several days: cool, calm,
quiet, dank, breath, heart,
and figured a way that rain
might make the trees purr,
but the noun 'puddle'
has given me the most trouble
for the ink from my pen would run
and my pencil would not write at all
on the wet paper.

　　　　　　Come winter,
I shall write of a snowfall;
the white of Premium Copy 24lb,
should give little hindrance
to pen or pencil, under dry snow.

Old Woman in Country Winter

Out of her hourglass filled with memory
now half empty with forget
and laden with December,
falls,
from the grace of clouds in a winter's shroud,
a caked and wedded icing over chequered fields.
Over dawn a land reborn in style
coddles the farm in downy dreams.
Its drift,
blown to the hedgerows, in a woman's curve,
cottontails the hatted house in gingerbread.
The morning blarneys the blushing barn,
its wimpled roof once handsome and metal'd.

Pristine, the ermine land invites
the ditched and foraged fox,
footsteps along a dotted line
his sign.

How little the pen has colour over cold?
Not so the page.

Close silenced, by the distant earshot-wind,
the snow-perched sparrows.
Even the chocolate stream,

                                lucid,

crochets quietly on its icing pass.
And clement, a sun-made photo-sky,
all clear to Aldebaran.

      In this Elysium,

                            quiescent,
      out of a firmament of blistering stars
and forever-rampant gravities, space curls away
as though it knows *she* is the centre of *her* universe;

      safe from the neighbouring wars,
                  caught in the brief of morning glory
      —an interlude of loveliness
that nips her fingers and consumes her heart.

Poem Written from the Inside Looking Out

The first lines of this poem
I plucked from the sky
while the sun was called away;
they were loitering among clouds.
I have laid them between hills
under the word for 'tarn'
so that they will not billow
should the wind blow,
though a hindrance of beech trees
forms a wind-break to the north
which, in the interests of the poem,
I assembled from a small coppice.
Little girls are picking wildflowers
further down the hill;
I would have preferred them,
in deference to the poem,
to have been paddling
in the shallows of the tarn,
but felt it much too much to ask.

Before Feet and Inches

the oceans were scanned
in crests of waves
the heaths in sprigs of heather
and the weight of thought
was measured by
the heft of a single feather
Springs were counted in irises
the set of summers in sun
the height of sky
expressed in stars
and the pebble by nail of thumb
A living was reckoned
on winter's breath
and in increments of stillness
                              death

S.J.W.

I am S.J. the photographer
merchant of light
catch your sun second-hand
freeze dancers quicker than ice
stop history in its tracks
ten thousand times

queens, princes caught
in full reign
each image no more
than a taste of death
yet in a casket once
I brought a man to life

I take your look, your like
what the sky gives
fix it on the retina of pasts—
so many eyes bequeathed
to follow the world
that give a glimpse of leaving

Matter Seen Through the Window of Heaven

I know nothing of violins but there is something
seductive about their geometry that piques curiosity
and so, on an impulse, I paid him what he asked.
It might have been a Stradivarius,
for there is luxury in ignorance,
but I hoped not, for then I would have
to choose my own comfort over its ownership.
I could not bring myself to take it out of the case
at first, reveling in its novelty:
its aging varnish, the quaint curls of the scrolls,
the very excitement of its form.
I knew I would never play
for I have heard maestros, of advanced age,
who did not play well.
It was lighter than expected
and I nestled it under my chin
as I have seen others do who can make it sound.
Resting the bow, I was afraid to break the silence,
and lost in thoughts of Oistrakh, Francescatti,
imagined the pure delight—
                    in the sunlight of Mendelssohn.
It rests now, propped tastefully in the chair
beside the window where nobody ever sits.
Nothing I own has a more sublime imaginable.

Author's comment:

All my life I have wanted to play the violin,
but now at the age of 92 I have had to put the ambition aside
along with climbing Mount Everest (on a warm day),
and wanting to join a circus.

Where Quiet the River Avon Flows

Methinks, from out of the complexity of words
Shall come to now, proximity of an earlier time
As if from then my youth's coincidence of where,
And his youth too, before the headiness of fame
Rumoured his Warwickshire, its fields, its lanes.
I know his church, its clerestories, tower and spire
And many'd the span of arch red-brick, across his stream
That winds in company about this path, knowing the lore
Of cottage thatch, half-timbers, and of wattles daubed,
The Dingles, Charlecote, Shottery, and the Arden wood.
Did he meander here with Mary, ride with John
And later, breathe to Anne of Venus and Adonis
Where I, in his midsummer nights, have dreamed
Under his moon, his stars, his firmament?

Wife of Many Seasons

I cannot hold you in my words,
swift shadow of a tiny bird:
my lines the whisperings
        of paper dreams.
Of stroke and serif
I would build a garden, for
        I must tell of you
as quill'd papyrus told
        of venerable queens.

Oops

I set the glass of wine down
on the word for table
and watched it fall
on to the floor, for
although the floor and
the glass of wine were
in the world of matter,
the table was in
      the world of thought.

Jigsaw with Pieces Missing

I prefer a lone star on
   a clear night where the
dark comes in slowly

sprinkling the fields
   with dusk, and Sirius,
with the fishes in the

pool, twinkles like a
   pickerel's eye and day
hands off its petulance. This

evening, it happened while
   I read your poem; the
failing light turned all the

page to words as though
   a breakthrough might
reveal the heart of it—would

set us clear, would set us
   free from all attachments, and
lost in the revealing dark I

stood beneath the willows
   —still one bright star pointing
a bewildering direction.

Ode to a Drunken Fruit Fly

Mainly, I buzz fruit
and when this giant hand comes at me
I was ready for it and dodged
but it caught me a glancing blow,
and down I went straight into the glass.
I recognized a pleasant enough red;
a Grand Cru Burgundy, I think
though it could have been a Sangiovese
—a decent enough nose, adequate length
a modest palate and a cheeky little finish.
They say your life passes before you
as you drown but all I can recall was
an impressive profile of blackberry,
cassis, cedar and spearmint,
and as I went down for the third time
I was struck by how the layered
spice notes combined with balanced tannins
and acidity to have produced a true red
that would have been a classic pairing
with prime rib, beef wellington,
roast lamb or venison.
I'm not much of a swimmer
but eventually got my water wings
under me and managed to surface.
It was a rough go I can tell you;
lord knows how many mouthfuls I took in
before I fly-paddled to the side.

For the moment, I was a bit dazed
and somewhat sozzled, but okay,
till she decides to take a slug. Lord,
how I avoided going down with it, I don't know.
Only the sticky lipstick on the rim saved me.
Strangely, the experience was quite sexy;
as the wine went down in the glass,
I was able to cling to the side.
Then she decides to top it up, then top it up
four or five times an hour by my count.
Each time, I take in a few more mouthfuls
and desperately try to avoid hers.

I guess I must have passed out;
next thing I know it's morning.
I'm lying in the dregs of a Grand Cru Burgundy,
or could it be a Sangiovese?
All is quiet except the pounding in my head.
Ugh, and that dry feeling like cement dust
in the back of my throat.
I'm a bit woozy, flap my wings,
dry them out a bit,
do a couple of laps—so far so good;
not too steady on the figure-eights but
ready to buzz the fruit again 'cept there is no fruit—
just empty bottles of booze and full ash trays.
Ooooh, and a rumpled stocking and somebody's bra.

God Musing

Should I, in an idle moment, take a day
bathe it in the warmth of gentle sun
then, over an undulating weald,
lay a patchwork quilt of fields
and, to put the rustle in a breeze
a handful, here and there, of trees
and where within the quilt, a seam
as from a dell, or better yet, a spring,
a rivulet that babbles in a stream
down a dingle-wooded fell
            then for resting and relief
over tree-lined lanes a cloak of velveteen
beneath infinities of stars, a solitary moon
and in between, a dawn to warn of morning
and in the wane of afternoon, a dusky light
before the inevitable totality of night
    but for fear of mankind's wilful harm
    I leave it all for lovers arm in arm

Perspectivus

In late Indian summer's set
delft-like a speckless sky
spans a sun'd and Sunday morning land
where flowery as these words tie-dyed
the trees shout out Ontario's October
where I ramble ancient miles of fields
and in a clearing stumble
on a yard of fallen stones
now vandalized by time
that razed the nearby village too
and left headstones beheaded
prone amongst the grasses
so they lie as those for whom they speak
And so I tread and read precarious
their weathered names and times
the niceties of love leftover
sad words for such a sunlit reverie
now out of mind and almost out of sight
for none come here and yet
it is an hour of precious solitude
and noted the mere compass of their lives
their meagre age of no more
than a hand of years

no greater tragedy than dying young
for these were the children
of consumptive and of typhus times
and in the wonderment
of now and here and me
I hoped that they had lived as I have lived
at least one perfect autumn day

Gaia Reads a Palm

I see footprints of bare feet
sun-baked along a beach,
    she said,
hear the clang of iron on iron
scent the odour of stables,
    she said.
Somewhere a woman sings
in an unknown tongue
and a hand lights five candles—
Do you taste honey?
    she said.
And from the cusp of a moon
a dream in twilight hangs.
Oh dear, I see ashes,
    ashes, she said.

Pound's Rihaku

Lament of the Frontier Guard.
The River-Merchant's Wife: A Letter.
Exile's Letter.

What did they say of you, Li T'ai Po
those kings and princes
of momentary fame and soon forgotten;
did they say
no poet's words would sound
through thirteen-hundred years?

You wrote in commonplace
of love and war, unquestioned,
compounding loneliness with journeys

that we might know Rihaku's name,
the guardsman's sorrow,
the village desolated in the wake of war
and winter coming.

That we should eavesdrop on the merchant's wife,
a woman-child in love awakening
who loiters for her husband on the river Kiang.

That we should read the exile's letter to So-Kin
and know of Rakuyo, Hei Shu, Ten Shin of Cho-fu-sa
aware of all these places said and read
buried now beneath the wait of centuries.

Just a Few Stones

A hallowed place
I go there for the loneliness
Nowhere surrenders
so much to the sky
Still the hill fort contours
and the later desecration
leave a hint of the sword
a sliver of the church
yet the blood of history
has dedicated
a peacefulness

August Thought

This space in which
a summer takes its time
green and open time
the friend of fields
outspread as arms
that welcome sun
this trip of days that open
wide as sesame and close
in turn ambrosial quiet
nod bless of nights
take them these times
they are the gods
they are the understanding

Music Hall

Sex is something
God has thrown in to ensure
we do not confuse ourselves
    with deities, with angels—
a kind of tether
that never lets us stray too far
from freshly turned earth after rain
and in the pathos of it all
a constant reminder
    of vaudeville, of burlesque.

In a Tramp's Time

Rain, rain and on the rain's
sad-sodden moor
he breathes the breath of clouds.
And in the weather's raw

and watered mouth
sighs bacon-sizzle sound
of day-drool day,
wringing its metaphor

in tears from summer
writing winter's rain.
As this Northumberland's
December draws

unsheltered miles;
not ditch nor even hedge
not hint of time
of any century, for sure,

from out the drizzle day's,
mist-mizzle night,
he falters on the oddments
of the Roman wall

turns west for Banna,
makes for Birdoswald,
   —warmth, the hostel-line
    and sweet furmety

At Ninety-Two

I live the drear cortege of days
my midnights never far from noons
and in the tatters of my life
inhabited by drunken moons
the sky, the clouds, come drifting in
and slow my talk.
I take my words from requiem,
the hours, the days, are heavy now.
I take my walk from men too long at sea.
We must be who we are, and when,
and this is me.

The Lady Yang

On hand for the mace of offices, she tired of the
purple-capped *cockmen outside the red bird gate
until, wasting in a garden on a morning-tongued
poem by Shang-Yin, she was singled out,
in a fortune of red candles, by the Master of Robes
as concubine to the harem of Prince Shou
out-bedding his wasp-waisted women
with their insignificant accoutrements
to fall plump-pink in her ripe-plum days
hips abundant, into his **Emperor father's first favour
where she took him in his age and disabilities
raising the phoenix from his ashes to the clouds
of the white city, where always she could make
the spring rain fall in his sixty winters.
In reward, he made her Empress and gave
her a golden room in a palace of twelve towers
and nine, nine-fold gates
where she ruled with the Emperor's right hand.
Now, she is carried by litter from the gardens.
Five crows watch from the bamboo grove.
A winter that took the Emperor will soon take her.
            Neither will leave a deathless reputation.

*Men who announced the break of day
** Hsüan Tsung

In a Nutshell

I sit here, in a quiet room
no noise from the fridge
the furnace silent
and for the curiosity of it
I turn off the light

now at the mercies of touch
of taste, and of smell
there is not enough space
and too much time
for my life is of no more
than an arm's length
I do not know of stars
or of Wordsworth's reaper
 singing

my epiphanies but
ambrosia on the tongue,
the fragrance of a rose,
and only,
     shall I know love now
             by the touch of it

Homo Sapiens

Once we saw
but no more
than a cave of us
and then a tribe,
a village, town,
a city, state
—until today
our talent shows
a world of us
and we
    are mortified.

Conversation with a Sleeping Wife

What was this fantasy
through which we played
the hours, the years,
touching on friendship,
where daisies blossomed,
enveloped in love?

What of that blackbird
that sang in the dead of night,
the primordial of the first kiss,
the charm of intermezzo,
delectable nuance of fine wine.

How we savoured them all,
and so, while I can,
I say, Good Night my love
for in mystery we came,
without heraldry shall sleep.

Iter

As of some long forgotten youthful quest
I stood summered in this afternoon of fields
along this streetly path from once Caerleon
most overgrown and far from any byway now
dreamy in some quiet and country hide
to nowhere's remnant of an empire derelict
where once I maybe from some Celtic llan
journeyed on this fare to Ariconium
with a burden of remembered words
fancy fable, rhyme, lore, stories of songs

Water Meadow

How gently the wisps of sky
touch the brush of trees,
the grasses sing quiet descant
to the murmur of the stream.
There is a reverence here,
reminiscent of a sigh or a tear
a purity untouched by any hand
yet in the hedgerow, a stile,
worn by the touch of many hands,
for whom it's history
           is their epitaph.

The View from Here

In particular, it is of the agèd, those who
have lived to understanding, that I write
not of those, who in their carelessness
and in pursuit of importance, chanced youth
to isms, rogues, gods or celebrity.
I stand not as the purveyor of wisdom
but as the chronicler of comings and goings
and speak for those who have escaped
the fad of times and have taken all the care
to live forever and now wait patiently
in the expectation of the unexpected...
something falling from the sky perhaps.
No, likely a more insidious coming about
within the silence of the flesh, unwitting,
that bargains in the fickleness of time
with all the unimaginable of possibility,
while they, blithe, go on, make small talk,
scorn, shun, fancy, favour here and there,
on trifling days, bring home a loaf of bread.

Magician

In those days things was so quiet
folks came running
even for the snake oil men
so when she heard the wagon
was in town all coloured up like a rainbow
and with the painted heads of beasts
some said kept changing,
said they was lions others said they was bears
I guess she was bored
for she pretty well dragged me
down to that patch a dirt next to Ansel's place
where this wagon was parked
the whole side opened up
to form a stage on which he was
already sharping cards, pulling eggs
out of children's ears
and so there was quite the crowd
before he got the whole damned
shenanigans under way
what with the white rabbits
flimsy coloured scarfs the length
of a goddam fence and the collected nickels
that kept on disappearing
oh yes he passed around the hat
and he had the crowd in his hand
if you can ever say that about
a magician but by the time he came to

his *pièce de résistance* as he called it
though nobody knew what that meant
he needed a volunteer
do I have a pretty young lady from the audience
he said and before I could stop her
she was gone first up on the boards
where he takes her back of the stage
for a minute or two and when next I sees her
he's got her all done up in this scanty outfit
tassels sequins and would you believe tights
and all the fella's was a whoopin
and I can tell you I didn't like that
and I was ready to slug a few of em
when James Workman puts his hand
on me shoulder steady now he says
and I had to admit when I sees her
I feels like whoopin meself
steady now says Jim and before I knows it
this fella's shuttin her in this here box
and pushing swords through her
but she ain't hollerin nor nothing
so I spose she was orlright
then with a mouthful of mumbo jumbo
and in a sudden hush that falls over the crowd
he throws open the box and she's gone
just like that and all that's in the box
is a solitary white dove
that flies off into the blue over Fargo's place
there was a smattering of applause
then the whole caboodle folds back up
into the side of the wagon

and they all drifts back home to their suppers
leaving me and this coffin of a box
with all these animal heads what keeps changing
I couldn't figure if they was bears or wolves
the danged thing had no doors and I banged on its sides
and I shouted to her but there was nobody in there
he'd gone she'd gone
I figures maybe she's back out at our place
and I makes me way back to the edge of town
but she's not there neither
so I hurries back but by now the wagon's gone
some said they saw it
all four horses going hell for leather
on the track to Silver Springs
others swore there was but a yoke of oxen
and they was headed out Karpov way
yet others saw only one nag pulling the wagon
on its way to Suanita Gulch they said
so I borrows Dobson's horse
and follows their tracks in every direction
but never found a hide of them
people were decent about it
but I knew behind my back they said
she got fed up with Jed
left him for that fella's city-slicker folk
but to my face they said she'll come back Jed
once she gets tired of him
but me I wasn't so sure for nobody could explain
why every evening just afore nightfall
a white dove flutters at my window.

Out of the Sameness of Evenings

In a city, somewhere,
a street lamp and a bench
 —wrought iron;
that much I remember
from the way the leaves
dwindled into darkness;
her hat, a cloche I think,
rimmed in contre-jour,
left her face in shadow.

All this relived in sepia
somber of autumn
from similarity.

We spoke . . .
of what, I cannot say
 —trivia
the weather perhaps.

We did not touch.
She did not sing to me.
Yet I was left a captive,
my thoughts in chains,
wishing the days away.

The Sun and the Rain

The years in afternoons of summer drowse
hush quiet the treetop breeze a fiddle sigh
the honey'd humming's whistle down of larks
between the meadow hedge and barley mow.
Gone the silent summer half-past noons
the country ale, rough cheese and broken bread
the skirr of honing stone upon the scythe
the swing, the swath, the toil of reaper-glean
the sheave, the fork, the heave to haycock's lie.
Until the placid dusk meets wane of day
where you walk weary comfort on my arm.
We turn about the stile into the lane.
The hollyhocks a stone's throw from the door
where under the remember-moon we sleep.

Homage to My Muse

what songs she sings
in journeyed climes
under the roiling clouds
show caw-field wings
of black burnt crows
that float on a wind's rush
over the windrows

where a mind takes
upon itself wild rides
through endless canyons
of sunset wakes
marvels the spires
of a shimmering city's bide
lost as of ancient Tyre

and in a knight's night too
where a moon moon's
a wreck-green sea serene
salted with islands two
like opals in a milky whey
while lark-quiet hills rejoice
in the break of a late soirée

till her night mind winds
down a morning's might
on a rainbow dream queen's
wreath and chalice vine
to sounds of a starting knell
—a write time's waking
in the meadows of Asphodel

Fruit Fly

Fruit fly on a winter window
you are lost
skating on your frosted pond
turned edgewise.
Adrift in alien space
you flit, turn tiny loops,
know circles;
your smattering of atoms
confusing light for warmth,
sweet breath of ripe plums.

A Place that Language Made

The ruffled heather-broods
abound the Yorkshire moors
as caught beneath a moon
between uncertainties...
a rumble-country winds
the caried stone of crazied paths
about a place of Urra, Cringle,
Roseberry Topping, Lilla Howe
wherein the void of loneliness
emphasized by morning dark
whispers of history on the wing
in a value of lost tongues—
hallow this place of nowhere
       made of somewhere
              by the word

Footpath

I journeyed in thought
by way of path and stile
from Wheatley Green,
to Mellow's farm.
In the memory of youth
the day was willow,
the sky, a robin's egg.

The larks sang to me
softly as falling leaves
on a sliver of wind.

I walked in the footsteps
of maids, of swains,
of priests and kings,
as in the fields
a tranquility of light
that heaven has touched.

This was my falling
through the novel of history,
the foreword of my destiny.

Eye Site

When the eye doctor
looked into my eye
through his usual
paraphernalia
he saw the fields
from yesterday
and the elegant
display of azaleas
that had caught my eye
along the lane even,
at my retina's edge,
the few fragments
of last night's TV

Do try to rid your mind,
absolutely, of all thought,
he said, almost as though
he were a psychologist

Thought Before Language

I am here before your words
your talk, your language
before you split my world,
once whole, including stars,
into your lexicon
of teeming fragments—
how by words you ripped apart
my single thought
so that you think in pieces now
separating many stars from one,
many worlds from one—
but how in poesy's need
you struggle desperately
to reassemble
that you might think once more
as I did then, your world as one

Return

in element of fire
to then to them
down from trees
through
woodsmoke fear
to fire
the burning log
their man-made star
essence of day by night

past fanfare flames
the world of embers
breathes ash-grey
the firefly night
to cat's-paw crimson

who has not stared
eye bright and burning
from the dark
into
that glow world time
Neanderthal?

Nightlife

Sometimes, in a dream, I slip out to have a quick smoke.
I'm careful, keep a sharp look out—try that furtive look
that goes with goofing off. The other night I tried it
in a dream about sheep herding...satyrs, nymphs,
that sort of thing. Snuck behind a tree, surprised another fella
attempting the same game. He was dressed as a French
nobleman a bloody stump where his left hand used to be.
Thank god you've come, he said, in Cecil B. DeMille French,
I've been trying to light my siga. I had a lighter in my smock
so I lit it for him and we had a smoke and a lengthy chat.
His wife had left him, he said, which might have been why
he was dreaming he was in the French Revolution.
Yes, I said, my wife left me too which was likely
why I was dreaming I was herding sheep. I gotta go, he said
all of a sudden, I'm due to be guillotined in fifteen minutes.
I gotta go too, I said, sheepdogs are savaging the nymphs.
But we swapped e-mail urls. We are having a coffee together
if ever we get out of this damnable dream.

Entry to a Fifth Dimension

Cross first the meadow
in which you hear the lark singing,
turn to the willows
and the stream will point you
to a coppice on a hill.
You will know it from the gallows-tree.
Here, you must wait for an April,
follow its evening star on a clear night.
It will lead you to a hollow of dreams.
Choose but one, and in your reveries
follow the butterflies...

An Old Man Buys the Remnants of a Model Sailboat from a Thrift Store

Once some young fellow's fancy
in disrepair and fallen now from fashion
in the fickleness of mind and years.
Perhaps buried decades in a steamer trunk—
a dereliction of sticks, rags, string
donated in a toss between
a thrift store's charity and out to trash.

Now passing through some dozen hands
it triggers thoughts of now and then—
perhaps young Andrew, nephew Dwight
would like... until a second thought
would answer no, it's junk, it's too far gone;
better buy a plastic job from Toy's 'r' Them.

But then, as other old men might recall
the round and comfortable girls of youth,
this man minded curvature of boats:
a fair line on a clear run in a time of shipshape
and saw in her what once she was,
more than a diversion on a summer's afternoon,
more than the envy of park ponds and other lads,
more than the pride of the uptown boy from Keilly Way.

Taking her parts in parts
patiently he worked away her years
for she was of his time
his fingers only slightly older than her curves.
He smoothed and touched with brush
the oil and varnish, sewed the cordage, canvas
till her hull was spruce and set with sail
in geometric shape to shame the sky

> yet left enough of 1930's too
> that all should know
> when both of them were young.

Author's comment: As a life-long sailor
this model of gaff-rigged sloop
reminded me of early sailing days
on the Norfolk Broads.

Dome from Gore Assurance

Now it is set upon a fragility of straws
to look down from High Park
upon the old Galt
and the detritus of its contemporaries.

Under this dome
many spent their best years
amidst a mind-numbing abacus of numbers.
Numbers which,
in their conspiracy with likelihood,
lifted all suspicion of iniquity
from the shoulders of the Company
while it turned a profit
on the exigencies of life and death.

But what of the building...
how little of the character of a king
may be fathomed from his crown,
leaving this crown "stillstanding"
like a memory without a time.

Stowaways

It is as though I packed them all
in my suitcase before I left
...the fields carefully folded,
hedgerows, feel of wet grasses,
streams, hills, valleys, carefully packed
between the folds of a woolen sweater,
smells of the seashore, a waterfall
and even the taste of rain.

All lay quiescent, patient, till the
fast declining years gave their consent
for them to frequent dreams,
        inhabit day dreams.

Ruined Church on the Welsh Marches

Going, this once holy and neglected place
where briar, brush, leaf and nettle now,
given the weather's reign, predominate
Left leaning under the rise of a thicket lea,
the village gone its wattle daub to years
Only the church remains to be stumbled on
The lichened stone holds being, brokenly
where ivies hang from mullions frail
Fallow, the rood loft, tangled osiers now
that listen down the choir, a chancel wind
and the once-belled tower betides an oak
where, in its time, screened louvers pealed
Chirch or church or chirche, Celt or Angle
no matter neither not quite one or of the other
—pagan to Christendom, pagan back again
Slow, long, far the fabric of a space will fall
when no longer needed for its complicity
in yearn for shelter, comfort and fraternity

Prelude to an Epitaph

Four score years
approaching five
and dwindling

this unfathomed manufactory
assembles thoughts
from the demolition
of a lifetime's dream

Head, heart, belly, loins
and fragments of the boy
the youth, the man

fashion requiems
for mad coyotes
    baying to the moon

Day Left by a Suicide

Up before dawn I enter the world
through pages of the *Morning Standard*
leaving it for dry toast and tea
as the sky comes in through my window
bringing a tepid day with a touch of winter.

I follow my nondescript hat, coat, shoes
out into the lane taxing the morning with walk;
I carry the hill for a mile or two.
It is heavy, and resting it, I look down
to see them, tiny in cars, on buses—
factories, shops and offices moving towards them.

The morning passes in its usual tedium.
They are in cafeterias by noon ordering coffee,
Danish, fries, while the sun, in its omnipotence,
dusts the sky of what little cloud,
and stretching its legs, the afternoon
rests uncomfortably on what is left of morning.

I look down on St. Swithins in the Fields
but there are no gods on Thursdays,
and passing lifeless, the day slopes
to the familiarity of four o'clock.

Forsaking this hill to the inevitability of gravity
I shall carry evening back to my room.
Through my window the sky will leave again
and in the forget of darkness
I shall drink wine, more wine, more wine,
            till even the moon weeps.

Blue Night Leaving

Five is the hour
for the want of silence;

where the baritone bullfrog
at the hint of light
lows, no... no... no.

and over the wood, in scissor'd song,
a hundred birds in a frenzy guess
at the prodigal sun's return

and the indeterminate sounds
of the preyed and the preying
have left in the play of night

and undisturbed,
in customary themes,
the poet dreams,
wasting another dawn
for the want of words.

El Niño

November daffodils in bud
Antarctica has turned to mud
Elephants in icy glaze
Arctic Circle cattle graze
On Everest in tepid pools
Piranhas swim in piscine schools
North blows south and east blows west
Inuit are over-dressed
The English give a rousing cheer
There are no showers though April's here
While farmers don't know who to blame
For only Queen Elizabeth's reign
Chad is raining cats and dogs
Algiers is lost in London's fogs
Even the ancients don't remember
A heat-wave in Nome in late November
Torrential rains submerge Death Valley
Grass-skirted bottoms freeze in Bali
Wool undies from too-brief bikini
Change with the magic of Houdini
Night-and-morning-red-skies tricked
Even shepherds can't predict
Nor can Grandma's rheumatism
Foretell tomorrow's cataclysm
The sunny side of every street
Is blanketed by snow and sleet
Cairo Fatimas shake their bellies

Ridiculous in English wellies
No longer are the plains in Spain
Talked about as having rain
Kilimanjaro's snow capped peaks
Have not had snow on them in weeks
Del Fuego's Williwaws
Are blowing hard off the Azores
The sun sets in the afternoon
Surprised when autumn falls in June
Singing in the rain is out
Gene's now dancing in a drought
Camels slosh through desert muck
Thirsty is the waterbuck
Canadians in their quandary
Leave for Lebanon to ski
Distant heavens jabberwock
Cloud battledore and shuttlecock
Skittered by the spin-drift wind
Whether genie'd weather ginn'd
Contrary-wise the clockwork sun
Suggests that God is having fun
The last time that he pulled this lark
We needed Noah and the ark

At Less than Arm's Length

I know you feel my kisses, love
and still, I know
the softness of your hands.
You share the river
of my thoughts.
Lie peacefully, my love
for I am with you
in your twilight sleep.

Clockwork

Momentous as the find of fire—
timing the turnings of great suns.
First, fragments of the hour
dim-glassed in sand
then turn of shadows then
came the work of clocks
(that made redundant, journeys
of the sun), telling in hours, in
days, in years, of life and death and
predicating noon that tea and buttered
scones were punctual at four-o-clock.
And late the word *late* came
and *early* too would complicate as
every soul gave up its timelessness
for Time from each was taken
and given *tout le monde;*
to all is *then,* to all is *now*
—a regimen imposed
the chains of happening,
and all would run eternally
to race the falling phantom
grains of sand

Old Man's Recollection of a Seashore

In sob in heave in yomp and swell
the bellied tide high neap and ebb
pregnant's a seawall's netted greens
rides shoal mole bulwark groin
tolls the briny knell of sextant sea

Gull-wise the sun-warmed touch
calls listens at the jetty'd shore
of children's summer sounds
foam froth spume wash
and wishes sibilant reclaim
the undertow three four five
cries of night-watch gulls

For these are the night years
of lifetime's treats and tears
the wave-break-wrinkled moons
spindrift the age of anchorage
of flotsam and of jetsam thoughts
the age of last rememberings
in a living of sea songs

Ever the crab-tide pelagian shells
throng teem habit limpet pools
where late the children of the sea
in the play of castled sand a
bliss laugh joyance and delight
of they who lubbered watched
the beach-run dare-tot-child
toe-trip the in-come tiers of tides

Do you not hear the sea singing?

Life Signs
of Neglected Sparrows

Write in your natural style
they say, whoever *they* are
"An ordinary workaday
voice dressed in its Sunday best.
Poetry is casual;
words should fall like snowflakes."

But what if you mince words—
wander purposely amongst
the tombstones of dead poets,
wear ruffles, frills, a tutu,
dress as the Sun King
—make snowmen
of the falling snowflakes?

What then?
See a life's words rise in the
smoke of next-of-kin bonfires?
No! Bury them in a cookie jar
these poems,
to be found in a century or two
like the skeleton of a child
buried under an oak tree

Bury them
till the Emperor's New Clothes
are again in fashion

Burning of the Last Strad

Some poets said, it would go down in ice,
others said, up in fire.
Some said, with a bang,
others, with a whimper.

First the summers warmed more pleasant long and hot.
In the northern climes the winters lost their edge.
No one encountered snow in several hundred years.
Gradually each season lost its difference,
became a whole eternal suffocating summer.
The callous eye of nature, blind,
sucked each breath of moisture from the earth,
slaked lakes and rivers dust and boiled the seas.
Those dependent on the cold were first to go
others followed till at last were those
who, exhausting every source, succumbed.

In a cellar corner deep, at rest against a sandstone wall,
left by one who sought naïve redemption,
stood the last and only Stradivarius—
the Kreutzer maybe or perhaps the Davidov,
maybe played by Oistrakh, Paganini, Hahn or Sarasarti
and still in tune despite the holocaust.

Small blisters formed at first, ballooning large
until they burst and showered the stone with resin blood;
faint wisp of blue prevaricated flame and then,
matching the spruce display of varnish glow,
reached the eternal point between—
                        behold, epiphany of gold.

        Strange, the glory of it;
        is there art in crass destruction,
        craft reduced to fine grey ash as smooth as soap?
                What now the price of pride...
                            the odds of genius?

Wake of a First Poem

    Until that summer
spent with words
that fell upon the beat
of metronomes
of phrases tuned
to orbits of star-dreams
of cipher-salted stanzas
each a mote
    along a paper chase
    that followed Time
    down antiquated steps
    through hidden doors
      to poesy eloquent

Helhiver Line

Three of them in a meanlean month of a year's
mouthdown and outs.
Indianwinter's sharp for-ever-uary snaps
an early spring and traps two days,
and a third night uppencoming in the boxcar's,
boxpine'd cold,
uppencoming to a tune-town or so it loomered
in the halflight.
Soup-longing and bake-spud-ding warmth about their hands,
hot sweetening tea and a leaf out of the spring, they dreamed.

"I'll doubleyou tomorrow's freight," he hollered
to a huddled Mac, a numbled Weller-
"tonight I charm a roof, a girlybed, a shandytown," he said,
"and laughadollar's grub,"
and sliding the coldarm boxcar, boxcold, door,
he dropped on to the slowing curve,
legstiff with coldforced bodychasing into an almost fatal run.
He stood boxscarred,
watched the caboose ending in the fallen night,
clack-clack, clackety-clack-clack;
a distant dying whistlelike a mountain shouting doom,
leaving the wind to fill its silence,
leaving one cold for another and turned toward the
town and company.

Not much of places
cept the main street to-a-tee that braked abruptly
    at the tracks,
its devilfinger esselling the hill.
No sound, no sounding but the wind-blown-sleatly,
no light, no lighting but the remnants of the gonerday.
A charcoal stretch drawn on the black-nip-night.

He wondered strange and only:
had they turned in, turned in early sleepward?
Unkindly's taken to a vagrant's cursed-of-times
and kindess follows hesitant from wakensleep.
He wandered talkward to the footlings of a shack
and so the second and the third;
posthumus, an after-sound for eighty years agonerwas
and backed upon dalmation'd pyramids of slag and snow.

No grub, or warming girlybed;
a whore's frost makes a fool of idiots, he swore,
gold-arm, fools-cold, ghouls-gold,
weatherwained, highstreet deviant de-paved,
its traffic windwilled rust and corrugated tin,
ends abrush of scrapyear's scars,
            tree-wilderness, be-wild-er-bush.

Unexspectrer'd and macabre-a clapped-out mining town
 drawn ore to dust now filled with ghosts and not a
    shinglesingle roof.

Tall storied clapboard; once an office of the mine,
leased-hence-and-greased an escalator of a sort
lay drybone-laundered in the mangled iron.
Its wreck-and-floor now mimed a found-floor-roof
and frosted gunnystuffed the broken windypanes out of
    the treason cold

        and look, and luck—a rusting stove!

Cussed-and-kissed the girdling-iron down to a
    lastmatch kindledamp
made fire a miracle
but burn it did, the draffishstove to smokey mounting tune
of bubblingstud; half-heart-hearth, its stoke and
    drawry burned a glow
in pomp and circumstance.

Two-feet astove in everygarb his own and
starvelingwarmed his hands around the chip-enamelled
    mug's hot sweeteningtea.
Keptember in a frigid stare was deep in thawed and
    thinking nothing,
fretless, feckless of the late, wait, freight
that brings tomorrow's *now* and might not slow,
    and might not show
                —thinking,
    nothing-man can feel his god,
                and god knowing.

She Had Heard the Owl

It was me, Alton, Leofrick,
and Tom the smithy
who carried Hildred Windermere.
For Saint Patrick's church held
the burial rights for Berrywillow.
We took the Corpes Path
straight as a ley line
and were well on the lych way
to Kirk-way Field by noon.
She caught a fever...old—
must have been forty and kept a
witch bottle in every window.
By mid afternoon we had rested twice
setting the coffin down,
thankful for the corpes stones.
We hurried past the Comb Crossing
for fear of the God of Death.
Alton said we had crossed a cursuse
left by an ancient peoples.
We hurried on for fear of revenants
yet it was evening before we saw
the lych gates of the churchyard
and carried the coffin three times
around the graveyard cross.

Aelfric had the grave prepared
and after the burial proceedings
we paid the priest and left to find
ourselves a sheltered place to sleep
for we dared not risk the ghost road
after dark for fear of corpes candles,
Jenny Burn-tail, Joan of the Wad.
The night was silent. We Slept.

Once Around the Sun

As usual, spring came in
on the dregs of
the old year's winter
Came in like
a schoolgirl skipping,
but summer is its flower
The sandal days come,
one after the other, fast
as a waterfall of clocks to
the sudden halt of autumn
whose leaves in the wind
mimic the hush
of the late winter's need
    for a New Year

A Quantum Poem

And so I said to God
...then give me senses
so that I might know
the way it really is
and so God did and
I was the eye perfervid
quick silver in
the colours of a fractal time
nowhere and yet everywhere
was happen of creation
demolition and event
I watched the rocks
in their commotion
erode to sand and
like the days and nights
I saw the universe
wax and wane the stars blink
in the variant eye
of a never time and
I could see the chameleon
of forever where
once there was nothing
now there was something
and I could gather
atoms in my hands
letting them slip again
like lentils through my

fingers and I was privy
to whoever was
and privy to whoever will be
gone was the neat
familiar cube of commonplace
time-tidy order of things
we think we know
for there was no this or that
or now or then or was or will be
all was of an entirety
I was part of a star
part of a stable in Bethlehem
part of a woman in Uzbekistan
part of this poem

Quiet Thinking of an Immigrant Poet

The house on Mapleton with the iron fireplace
we all sat around each winter
Country lanes that led to everywhere
in a smaller country with less sky
The "in Ardens", the "on Avons",
the ford in Tanworth village,
the lakes at Earlswood
and underfoot 2000 years of a country's talk

All thoughts sandwiched between the touch
of a Harris Tweed sports coat,
the lingering smell of pipe tobacco, and
most now, subject to the inevitable ruin of time

Mr. Whittaker

He came with all the regularity of the afternoon
from god knows where: The Gospel Oak
The Three Magpies or The Horseshoe Inn?
Down the road he'd come, and turn into the grove.
I never saw a man so drunk yet still himself.
We lived at one-hundred and forty-four
Stapleton Road right opposite of the grove.
Nobody could come or go without us seeing them
and it was an agony...a fascination just to watch.
He started with an open stance as though
about to catch an enormous rubber ball
and then his upper half would fall off to the right
until his feet, in several frantic steps, caught up to it
coming, for an instant, to a halt short of the curb
where his upper half this time would fall off to the left
and another *pas de deux* of hectic steps,
then he'd stop and take a breather in the hedge,
his zigs, the zag bewilder of a failing heart
until he disappeared around the footpath's turn.
And so each afternoon we'd view a hundred steps
of Mr. Whittaker's long day and know that
for a pound a week he carried dustbins on his back
and emptied them into a waiting cart...
more than his work, his station in the class of things
said of him there's nowhere else to go, but up.

Between Two Solitudes

I

In a wild darkness that we do not see
a chaos of red giants, white dwarfs,
matter circling, doing what matter does
nova, supernova, heed the laws of stars
taking their own sweet nondescript time
where out the void of boundless place
—a dairy queen's vast Milky Way,
the magnanimity of a mothering star
and a sun-place of greenery with a moon
wherein this timeless gift of night
I delight in the call of whippoorwills.

II

Look at my hand, it too is a firmament
proton, neutron, quantum mysterious,
matter circling, doing what matter does
subject to the laws of fragmented stars
four quark Ds, electrons, neutrinos
and the charm of charm-strange mesons;
but in the immensities of a boundless void
sub-atomic birds might fly great distances.
My hand has all the wild'erness of stars
yet this is the hand with which I touch,
this is the hand with which I love.

As I Was Passing

Women danced the Charleston on the gravestones
    of the Kaiser's war.
Men waited in the serpentines for soup, for work,
    a second war, to fill their bellies.
A generation ripened.
Cities raised while nations foundered—awash in
    reigns of enmity.
And reckless victors reached for stars and seared the flesh
    of sleeping children.
                  All this I saw, as I was passing.
In the chill of victory the sphere was split.
Each hemisphere awaiting—will the other blink?
And the horns of beasts were ground to feed the lusty
    overcrowded world.
                  All this, I saw.
Sands were blackened by the silver of expedience.
Men looked for moons, launched planets, which beyond
    the skies
delivered pinpoint demolition, moved a word from lip to ear
    a half-a-world away.
Tongues would whisper to a half-cocked world,
while unheard in dark corners, children whimpered.
                  All this, I heard.

And one side blinked and both halves thawed.
And some had waited fifty years—had bridled the ethnicity
    of neighbours,
and like butchers, slaughtered.
And the world prevaricated.
And in return, like butchers, gave hearts
    and lungs and kidneys—
borrowed lifetimes from the dead to give the living.
                All this, I knew.
And so we climbed the steep millennium's zenith
as though it were the summit of a mountain.
But down this century's slope, still, men are falling, tripping
    on their mania for progress. We have lost the vision, lost
    the dream to comfort: too hot too cold too loud too soft
    too dark too light—at least—for Me—for Me—for Me!
And justice is confused with truth, and politics with sooth.
And the cracks about my bones admit to signals—
know the confines of mortality and remember.
Remember wading barefoot in the trout stream,
the dew-wet meadows in the morning window,
the larks at mid-year-midday-summer singing,
the midways in the summer's night-bright kernel.
Remember umber-peaceful sounds in country churches,
and strawberry girls afresh in summer-polka'd dresses,
and small boys playing.
                All this, I knew in passing where I danced,
                        oblivious, with a handful of the angels.

Afternoon in an Attic without Gravity

Skinny dipping in a wedge of amniotic dark
what ecstasy, yet beyond roof-ways the sun summers.
Strange how it warms without light
invisible sunbeams and me, a mote floating
adrift except for touch. I backstroke
touching myself all over for the hell of it,
feel the books float by as if by magic—inverted birds.
A portmanteau touches my leg.
What is it without its many labels.
Nothing here has form, has character;
magazines are kites quite useless, black on black.
A wedding dress floats by, a manta ray of heavy satin.
It envelopes me. I disentangle from its titillation.
Listen, there are sounds of heart beats.
Everything here is sensual; I must invite Cordelia,
what fun it might be, love is the art of touching:
space walk, space lie a mile high.
Quietly, quietly now, there is no sound
        except I sing softly:
                Where the bee sucks, there suck I:
                    in a cowslip bell I lie.

Figment

I took sleep
through the woods last night
stopping to watch fireflies
but there was more
than the mere space
that darkness makes...
a dream,
that took its mystery
from the delight of times
where love once tarried
extant
in all its wonderment
on its way to morning

Ann

Gently, I place her life
in a silver frame
along with her photograph
and a snippet of patterned silk
she had sought to make a quilt
but never finished, and
around its selvage edge, I tack
the fragments of my memories

Kenning

On the cadaver's heels of Rome they came:
Jutes, Eudoses, Saxons, Frisians, Angles,
amid shire-moot, ealdormen and hide hundreds
bringing their rune-stones in venerable whispers
vague unheard of, quiet unknowns mysterious,
across Seaxna, Hymbra, Englas, Myrl, and Rile
to set the *wil-sum* wonder of the modern word.
Cædman, Waldere, Cynewulf—corpus shadows
of the bards' five-centuries of lost loved labours,
spared a mere three-thousand words anonymous:
Dream of the Rood, Malden, Brunanburh,
Widsith, Song of Azarias, Elene, Deor's Lament
—tale-singing echoes from the age of darkness
yet their words survived the priss of Gaul
leaving us the likes of: bloom, chalk, aurochs,
sandal, seven, swallow, yew and candlemas.

(Œ) delightful

Grand River

How benevolent she flows wide and stately in the majesty of summer finery leaf-green awash with sky the murmur of her waters her streams obediently dividing at bridge and branch how she charms the countryside the trees bow to her the fields prostrate themselves to her gentle passing yet when the storm closed thickening the darkness like a second night I saw a different river from the mill the blacken clouds reflected in her face the millstream triumphant over the wind's roar hurrying the river's spume the weir a dark slash across the windy night and I thought of the boy in the innocence of childhood under the afternoon sun swimming when the river struck three days the weir withheld the man and the boy he tried to save three days till they were delivered from the river's belly and I thought of the years and the toll of the river's passing scarce a churchyard from Luther Marsh to Connor Bay without memory of the river's wrath and I shivered in the eerie dark and uttered a quiet prayer for them all

I Remember Antiosse

From the town we walked across the fields
on that late amble of an early summer's day.
This idyll lost on you, no doubt mislaid,
buried perhaps too deep in years and fortune,
but I remember you. How could I forget
the sift of surf, the cush of sand, the too-blue sky,
the still-warm bread they gave us at the inn,
the sharp and salty taste of Mimolette,
and the Bergerac; we drank a jeroboam, I think?
Almost biblical, we broke the bread, the cheese.
I remember you brought glasses for the wine.
What we might have talked of is long gone.
We sat and then we lay amongst the dunes
easy as if cradled in God's hands.
Perhaps it was the wine; too much,
and people do these things...and I remembered
in the half-light when we sauntered back,
unsteady, barefoot, in each other's arms,
you were singing Frère Jacques...or something
and I envied you your fluency, and feeling
you were still a part of me, I thought that you,
the world and me, would be forever.

Living Out the Dregs of a Long Life

As though from an upper window
looking down on a city's busy intersection
a man is crossing with the lights. It is me.
The driver in the car waiting for him to cross is also me,
on my way to the studio.
Later, a woman, opening an umbrella,
crosses in the opposite direction.
It is my wife, Ann, on her way to her office.
Early, the streets are flooded with sunlight
but as the morning staggers under the weight of traffic,
the afternoon takes over, trading the sunlight for shadow.
Ann is on my arm as we exit from Eaton's.
I have bought a suit. She has several shopping bags;
one contains a purse, another a winter coat.
Often, I see a small child holding her mother's hand,
then in the shopping bag there will be a doll or a pretty dress
that later, they will show to me.
The rush-hour takes over, leading the darkness
primed for entertainments, streets light,
car headlights establish their dominion.
I observe a couple leaving a restaurant.
I recognize "The Little Denmark" on Bay Street.
She is on my arm. We have dined
on the roast duck and a bottle of sauternes.

We walk to the Chevy, drive off.
Gradually the traffic leaves the streets to themselves,
there is little more to see,
so much has left along with the diversions.
As the pleasures played out, we paid the price in years.
Ann has left, gone home, and is asleep,
and as the years take back their dominance, as is their right,
I shall join her.

Thrift

I say to you but sky
you hear a sound
—one short syllable
that might have been
a quaver from
a blackbird's song,
and so you think in blue
of wisps of cirrus
in an endless light,
think in emptiness
of absent starless darks,
fancy, one short sigh
of sound, that signifies
the limitless of all
                              celestial

An Epitaph

I like to think
that she has left a star
and that shortly
I shall leave one too
for that is the way of leaving
so that when time
takes no account of clocks
or space, of foot-steps
for ever
we shall have a knowing

More than a Single Bloom

There is a place where I keep
moonlight, a rainbow and,
the sound of March across the fields.
Once on a daisy day, in a garden
a young girl is playing with dolls
and from an eon a starlit night where
barely the sound of a choir is singing.
A brush charged with aquamarine
takes a place amongst my thoughts
as though it is about to fashion
a gentle seashore seen from dunes.
There is resonance, waves lap gently
but also a wonderful quiet so soft
as to deny the authority of silence.
Do you not hear the planet breathing?
Tonight, I shall sleep with wild flowers.

Council House

Most will remember
the monotony
of crimson brick
but to me
it was the fire
the red hearth
in the black-lead
grate fire-bricked
for even more
economy
still so much heat
in one place
and nowhere else
centre of our lives
summer and winter
we talked
across the fire
and in the silences
listened to the coals
                singing

Gaia and the Mandrake

A milkmaid, barely seventeen,
who slept in Farmer Therrien's barn,
one April, walking in the fields
met an Ancient aged and worn
of curious physiognomy:
half man, part elfin, oddly sad
and from his ragged garment pulled
an acorn shaped distinctly odd.
Take this, my dear, the Ancient gave
(I have no further need of it)
and plant it in a covert place
that only you shall know and see
and tend it, give it honeyed-dew and sun
until a flower of indigo shall bloom
beneath a Manitoulin moon,
and with your hands—no trowel or spade
(he wagged a crooked finger) mind,
carefully unearth its root and bathe it
in a potion of fresh lavender and thyme.
When dried, then bury it in straw—
the very straw that makes your stable-bed.
With that, the Ancient turned and
with a twisted gait, half stumbled
off towards the settler's wood.

The maid, more curious than simple, took
the seed and planted it on Hemlock Edge—
a lonely soul-forsaken place near Portage Fall
that only the maid should know and see.
Indigo it blossomed, flourished, bloomed
under an August moon, the maid
with faithful fingers, fumbled (as he ruled)
no trowel or spade, unearthed the curious root
that bathed in fragrant lavender and thyme,
was dried like rosemary turned
      to droughty sun.

The root was curious as though
the earth had fashioned man in its design
its form was columnar, its colour wine.
The maid was true to the Ancient's bidding
and took the root and buried it in straw—
the very straw that made her stable-bed.

With harvest stir, the root was soon forgotten.
Though oft-times in her restless nights, reminded
as she rolled upon it, set it in her sleep, aside.

Until the eventide of spring, she wakened
from an idle slumber to a frenzy
—woke in paroxysms of wild passion;
not ravished, not assaulted, not afraid, but
charmed, enchanted, acquiescent, pleasured,
as if a prodigal—a lost love had returned,
and all their years of yearning came together
in a cluster like a galaxy of stars.
Then slept and woke as though it were a dream
and never wanted for another lover

   yet bore three sons
of curious physiognomy:
part man, part elfin, oddly sad,
who roamed the woodlands,
turned a furrow for their summer bed
   and stood solitary,
still as lofty maples, bowed
to winds as reeds and sedges do

as though a wife had fashioned men
of root and stem and leaf and flower
who spoke the language of the earth,
   and each winter, slept.

A Fly Is on the Window

I sit sipping a martini
before dinner
marveling at the genius
of Eric Satie's Gnossiennes.
A fly is on the window.
His music comes
the closest to poetry
...a linear melody
without need for background.
Is the fly in the room
or outside the window?
The music is inside my head
fitting into a mould
that is already there.
The fly flies past.
Yes, it is in the room.
A Glazunov symphony
is the next piece.
I love Russian music
but it is remote, distant, whereas
the music of France is in my head.
Always there is a familiarity
with the likes of Debussy, Verlaine,
the absinthe drinker
and even the Montmartre
ladies of the night.
The fly alights on the table.

Is it possible, that I am cognizant
of my genes' history?
The fly circles.
Why not? I know of
my index finger, and my nose
when it itches, not to mention
all my parts that constantly
remind me that they are there.
The next piece is by Delius.
The fly would seem
    to have disappeared.

Bothy in Northumbria

Can you sense this spoil of space
from the round of my words
after a day's trek from yesterday
how in the speckled light of dusk
a chill rain falls?

and lost, took a fool's turn
around five now miles off the wall
when out of nowhere's gloom
this cot looms menacing yet
a godsend of rugged stone and slate

A heavy door opens to arable damp
of earthen floor one window night-dead now
but a hearth with kindling
Strange this place so many miles
from comings or goings

I light my candle throw the specter
of my broken shadow on the wall
hard to imagine less comfort
yet a welcome haven
from a roofless world on a fireside night

I give prayer for he who left me logs
sit on my pack
eat bread left with luck from noon
drink sweet tea
for this is a place for thinking

and so I think until the fire burns low
till a stone ledge built for sleeping
hard but better than earth beckons
so I sleep and dream in groat-time
among the ghosts of shepherds

Adventures of an Aging Molecule

I reside behind his right eye—
have done so for most of his life,
an excellent vantage point.
No great urge to travel
apart from occasional jaunts
to a lobe here and there to listen in
on intellectual conversations,
though, now and then,
I yearn a holiday and mosey down
to a toe perhaps; I enjoy hiking.
Avoiding arteries, too much hustle
take the long way around the heart,
too hectic these days, the aorta
nose to tail a perpetual bottleneck.
So I travel leisurely by vein, avoiding
the area around the lower vertebrae
where hostilities have been taking place
for several years. I tire of his constant moans,
his attempts to rise from low chairs.
At the terminus where I must decide
to take either his left or right leg
I glance sadly out of the vein window
at the ruins of fleshpots where in my youth
I spent many wild enthusiastic frolics,
joined in his wild bacchanals.

I choose his right leg; to avoid delay
at his left knee from cartilage problems
and settle for a middle toe.
I have clothes for a week
and I hope to be back at his eye
for the Ibsen play he is taking in
                    that I want to watch.

Road to Harrisburg

Over the old iron bridge at Whiting's creek
that skirts the ghosts of Hezekiah's mill
unfenced, unhedged and open to the sky
a track that might be hidden from the road
spirals windless in a turn of curves
down rolling fields and trimmed by woods
where in the quiet, the hidden creatures doze
this hot and dusty summer afternoon.
Yet is there more to this exquisite calm
where I might laze as alders quiet as stone?
Is there more to this delight, an act of love?
Did cottage croft or village once stand here
share in a commonplace of kin
or in a passing family's perhaps
a child is buried on a somewhere's way
and in largess has left a legacy of love
to winnow down unfathomable time
held now in this hollow of God's hand

From a Poet's Notebook

(The poem before it is written)

The days deliver up the lines
as newsprint after burning.
Bright, wind-fanned, the edges
in trick-trickery of sound,
the fragments charred and rising
glimmer in the colours of the night;
the words in negative
black butterflies returning—

       As far away from youth as Mars
      the wryneck day sits waiting for the weather
      shouts from the other end of life
      in faded fashionable genes,
      urgent as horny in adolescence.

      And common as a crow's caw,
      the lettuce eaters seeking fame;
      fame fleeting as a quaver
           fame the rosy Carmenère,
              the hemorrhoids of time.

Stalked by the curvature of desire,
follows in the footsteps of slow women walking.
   "Tired of *always* in the een of smithers?
   Feeling lonely?
   Come and see me!
   Spend a green hour
   with the pixies in the dance."
          Doreen

In snippets of sound that filter down
a three martini buzz,
once dreamed of in the womb
and followed down the data trail,
writing on forest and forgot
the deadly never-green of gallows tree,
the noose of anodyne about the pivot
upon which years have turned.

Is it the man who blows his trumpet
on his knees and sees dim shapes—regrets
that should have taken place of dreams?

And in the silences, the loneliness,
the sound of Alph the sacred river
              running through the mind.
        Thought falls in simulcra—of mnemosyne,
        short circuiting the lightning nerve
        in the tunnel-vision-dark, womb-deaf,
        trading tears out of bronze forms,
        and well adjusted to madness,
        where, on the half-moon tide,
        beyond the veil of spin,
        a world is waiting.

And with the blinkered-frantic of a love-child sperm,
        thought falls
into the plasticine of language;
along with fat ladies and comedians
(slipshod souls out for the day in Eden),
a motley, clowning the mime of worlds,
the words come writhing,

sometimes for the sake of scenery,
sometimes sad as Sunday Schools between wars,
sometimes in the simile of smiles,
        the poems of the hourglass-empty rise
            full-fluted bubbling
                into the flimsy air of vanishing—

"words that speak to us like rain," Swahili say.

Spiral

There is something intrinsic
in the thought of a spiral staircase
that is perhaps akin
to the feelings of a child
on opening a new toy.
It is as though entering a nautilus
except for the feeling of wisp
as though it is loath
to take too much of air and light.
The intricate patterns in
the wrought iron add to its intrigue
as do the complex of the steps,
for nothing demonstrates more
the importance of the journey
over its destination.
And there is something heavenly
about running a hand around
the central pivot on the way down.
Could it be, subconsciously,
the mind expects to find a gene?

Redecorating the Living Room

You can never be yourself
you know
caught as you are
between fields and sky
gene of an ancestor
who used too much woad
was fascinated by stones
and slathered the walls of caves
in alizarin
like your African friends
who must have red

Last time
you used too much mist
and so you were lost
for most of the days

This time,
try to be nobody
let in the night if you must
drink tea to the sounds of owls

Adam's Rib

Look, you've got it all wrong,
it was hell on earth what with the Old Guy's
"Don't do this. Don't do that,"
and the signs, "Don't Pick the Fruit,"
"No Fishing," "Swimming Prohibited."
Bloody English Park Keeper,
with his "Keep off the Grass."
That's what he was
bloody English Park Keeper.
"No Clothes Allowed."
"Don't Pick the Daisies."
I ask you! And not even a please or a thank you.
Watched us like a hawk, he did
him with his bleedin' lightning bolts
every time you dropped a candy wrapper.
Why he was so upset over a few leaves
I'll never know.
Let me tell you, it was nippy in the mornings;
how would he have like to walk around
in the altogether?
And all those snakes he was so fond of,
creepy buggers, if you ask me.
Hey, and when I want somebody messing around
with my ribs I'll ask them, thank you.
Trouble was, there was absolutely nothing to do
'cept stand around looking perfect,
day after day, smelling the violets.

You've no idea how boring life could be
without sin, especially without original sin.
Let me tell you, Eve was a bit of alright
and I wasn't exactly low on the testosterone either,
though I say so myself!
I mean, who wouldn't have got around to a bit of
the old hanky-panky now and again
just for something to do, if you know what I mean.
But I'm still not sure why he threw us out;
I could tell Eve had been into the smokes again
when she said the snake tells her to pick the apple
—"Gw'arne, gw'arne," she said it said and so she did.
But I'd hardly taken my first bite
before we hears the Old Man screaming.
"Out! Out! Out! Out! Out!"
In a real tizzy, he was, so we hightails it
then he sticks a Hell's Angel on the gate
and that was that.
I wasn't sorry to be out of there,
I can tell you.

Perhaps Unnoticed

The night comes in
through my window
after another day of dust
How little of all happening
is worthy of remembrance
Yet some cut a swath
through history

Van Gogh, Mozart,
between sleep
and the drag of life,
found days of fortune
of beauty and of wonder
undimmed
      by any day of dust

Report Back to God

Their comings and goings
in the beginnings
left comfortable footsteps
They fused harmoniously
with the soil and its stone
but their insatiable creativity
gave way to a need for everything
and so, shrinking time,
they adopted their own evolution

Exuding toxins from
new arrangements of atoms
which trees should have provided,
employing the poisonous residues
of an earlier age
to facilitate more creativity and
fuel their need to go faster
and, in doing so, taking wing

The need for them to settle differences
feeble in their beginnings, now
involved the most violent forms of fire,
and continuing destruction of other species
on which they depended
further resulted in the sphere becoming
temporarily infertile due to
the infestation of Homo Sapien

There Will Always
Be Moonlight

Today's today is
the concern of tomorrow...
wake to a broken morning,
weather an afternoon
into the long road of evening
and nowhere's sleep...
wake to a broken morning
yet, take this world
from its downfall, pleasure
in the tranquility of memory
where, so much, that once
was *matter of fact*,
is now love

Light of Darkness

Now, the nights are
long, dark and quiet
as though
designed for caves
not like
the fly by nights that
in the blink of an eye
flickered through
my younger days.
Sometimes
in the dead of night
I turn on all the lights
just to
let the darkness free
like a bird, once tamed,
returning to the wild.

Contemplations on a Seashore

A place of *placidus* where
lovers lie amongst the dunes;
only sand and sky and
                    the sea breathing.
Under the while of stars
a honey moon turns
turtle from the sea,
and a dog-surf lapping,
two-times a lover's sigh.

Tomorrow's sun-child plays,
builds castles in the sand
learning trades
as did the likes of
Agamemnon or Boudicca.

And the sea turns on itself
in pregnant swells,
calls on the wind,
fools the shells and sounds
a chimeric roar that turns
upon its ear, the pride of men.
A gale force seven rising,
sounds the cries of gods
—Poseidon, Neptune's hurry,
                    and the kraken wakes.

Sea needs no albatrosses for excuse
to leave the tales of Crusoes,
Blackbeards, Darlings and Trafalgars
or fill its sea-chests with
doubloons, amphora, cannon rusting
                          and the souls of men.

          I knew this beach millennia ago
—came this way in Darwin's dream
          before the swinging pendulum of time
had rocked the crib of history.

In some draconian experiment
of sea, gill, air and lung we came,
amphibian in Trojan horse,
in legions from the sea, to take the land.

A pair of ragged claws, you say?
          I did not hear his mermaids
                    singing each to each!

Ode to Robert West

Onward Nineteen hundred and thirty seven!
              I am out of my mammy's home:
To wander in dark woodlands,
              Alone, all, all, alone.   RW.

You lie in Union Cemetery now, long years
your ragged body gone, yet amongst poets
still your imperative lives on, a monument
to progress failed, the ocean

Nith you sailed into the hearts of all
who crave the same untrammeled life.
A balladeer in errant time you lived
an otherways to greed and manic will.

We also, yearn your artless simpleness,
out of conformity the expected norm,
punched clocks, doffed caps to an absurdity
bend to the will of politician, mogul, fool.

And yet you made the simplest divine
in gentle, kind and natural demean that
taxes, callous trade and interest, seemed
mere attributes to pleasantries of dreams.

Do you still walk alone the Nith River's edge,
tread the dusky line between the day and night,
where fishermen or furtive lovers
catch your glimpse? That on your rounds you

might enchant a child, who, in the footsteps of
your time through worlds unspoiled
and tender on the threshold of modernity,
shall turn its back and not aspire a whit of it.

Son of Wally West, Bard of the Nith,
Robert (Bobby) West, of Paris, Poet, entertainer,
eccentric, died an old man in 1941.

The poem based on the historical essay "William and Robert West"
From the book "At the Forks of the Grand" by Donald A. Smith.

Midnight New Year

Ah, this fleeting instant's auld lang time
answers to bells obeys the clock-mime beat
in tribute to the power of common thought
brings the dime-stopped firmament to heel
all in a standstill moment's passing rite
to health acquaintance fare-well-fare
a toast to the constancy of all eternity
for this is a circle-celebration of the spheres
there is a round to it they did not fall
out of their prescribed and humdrum ways
and all the overwhelming odds star-point
these revolutions said of multifarious gods
will stay in motion's other-earthly reasons
and we shall turn another year of seasons

Dear God

Please, not under fluorescent lights
or in and amongst stainless, sterile things
about a fluster of people

or in the middle of a summer's day
(if it can be avoided).
The wrench would be too much.

Though, under a full moon
on a walk through a summer's night—
that would be altogether satisfactory.

But if I am to have my druthers
might I go, in a quiet corner somewhere
under subdued light and after a gourmet meal:
a Caesar perhaps,
pheasant in a blackberry coulis,
a glass of a good Chablis
followed by Crepes Suzette?
Then, just as I'm finishing a fine cognac...
(before the waiter brings the bill).

Oh, and God, just one more thing,
might you arrange for Kirsten Flagstad
to be singing, *Mild und leise...?*

Cordially,
Yours, etc., etc.

Index of First Lines

Stan White began life in Birmingham, England. He was an industrial photographer before coming to Canada in 1957 where he married and settled in Toronto working as a commercial and advertising photographer. In 1970 he joined Sheridan College as a teaching master and ran the studio for them for 20 years, teaching lighting and product illustration.

After he retired in the early 1990s, he continued with a life-long interest in stereo photography, photographing avidly in and around Brantford. These photographs are now in the local archives. In cooperation with the Photographic Historical Society of Canada, he set up a library of information on stereo photography now housed in the Art Gallery of Ontario.

Throughout his life, he has written non-fiction on various aspects of photography. In his 50s he began to write poetry and short stories. He has been published in local anthologies and has published several books of poetry, some in collaboration with other poets. As well he wrote a slim book on tabletop stereo imaging in 1970, *Beyond the Third Dimension*, published in the Netherlands and illustrated with ViewMaster reels.

These days, for relaxation, and in the hopes of slowing down the inevitable aging, he plays the musical saw and the theremin, but keeps the windows closed.

Visit his website: www.stanjwhite.com

www.ingramcontent.com/pod-product-compliance
Lightning Source LLC
Chambersburg PA
CBHW051341020726
47501CB00007B/2211